MY BIG BOOK OF
BIBLE
HEROES
DEVOTIONAL

GLENN
HASCALL

MY BIG BOOK OF
BIBLE
HEROES
DEVOTIONAL

SHILOH ⁵ kidz

An Imprint of Barbour Publishing, Inc.

Print ISBN 978-1-68322-361-0

Cover and interior character illustrations: Amit Tayal

Published by Shiloh Kidz, an imprint of Barbour Publishing, Inc., P.O. Box 719, Uhrichsville, Ohio 44683, www.shilohkidz.com

Our mission is to inspire the world with the life-changing message of the Bible.

Member of the
Evangelical Christian
Publishers Association

Printed in China.

05848 1217 SC.

CONTENTS

INTRODUCTION

The Bible is filled with stories of people who made mistakes. They were regular people who broke God's rules. But God loved them. When they obeyed, God used their good choices to help show them how to be godly heroes.

Spend some time with the heroes of worship, wonder, truth, friendship, and acceptance. Learn to ask God to help you link your obedience with becoming a hero. Ask yourself some questions to help each story really make sense.

The heroes in the Bible didn't become heroes on their own. Every hero had God's help. Every hero learned to follow because God promised to lead. Every hero was successful when they agreed God was in charge.

You might pick a few heroes you like. You might read some stories you can share with others. You might read about the qualities of some heroes and know that you will need God's help to be a little more like them.

The good news is, God doesn't want you to be just one kind of hero. God can help you learn to follow Him closely enough to be the hero of many different things.

If no one in the Bible had followed God, we would have no heroes to talk about. These heroes can encourage you because they weren't much different from you. They didn't always obey, but when they did God used them in some pretty incredible ways.

Become a hero today. No cape required.

1

From Worship to Wonder

Adam's Heroic Story

GENESIS 2–3

*If I tried to recite all
your wonderful deeds,
I would never come
to the end of them.*

PSALM 40:5 NLT

God showed Adam earth's first garden. Everything was new. Everything was beautiful. Everything was wonderful.

Water rushed over beautiful stones, birds sang the first songs, and the fruit was tasty. Adam was the first man, and everywhere he looked there was something so beautiful he couldn't help but smile. He was filled with wonder. He liked it.

You can discover wonder hiding in unexpected places. This might happen when you visit the Grand Canyon or Niagara Falls for the first time. Those are times when words like *wow*, *incredible*, and *awesome* are easy to say. But sometimes when you spend a lot of time with something fun, it stops being as fun as it was the first time. Instead of being excited, you might be surprised to discover that you're bored.

If you really think hard, you probably have toys you don't want to play with anymore. There may be places that aren't as exciting as they used to be. You might even ask your family, "Why isn't there anything fun to do?"

Adam is the hero of wonder. He's a good example of how to find it when you're bored. His secret? He used his mind. He thought about God. He saw beetles, flowers, blue sky, and hippos. Adam must have laughed at the monkeys, watched the birds make nests, and enjoyed the shade of a tree. He used his mind to understand that he couldn't make any of those things. God made Adam, and then He made everything else for Adam to enjoy.

It wasn't enough for Adam to just remember that God was the One who created everything he saw, heard, and tasted. Worship helped Adam keep wonder close. Worship is a way of saying that God is worth more than anything else. Worship happens when you say thanks to God, appreciate what He's made, and remember that He loves you. When you worship God, you don't have to play hide-and-seek with wonder. It can be found; it can be something you choose; and it can make a difference. Your mind remembers that wonder is much better than being bored—and worshipping God is better than being selfish.

Try to remember all the wonderful things God does. Make a list. Take time to say, "Thank You, God." Don't be surprised if you discover an amazing treasure called wonder.

*Dear God, sometimes I get bored. I'm not happy with things
I used to like. Things sometimes feel like a waste of time.
When I feel that way, help me remember that You made
everything. Help me think about how hard it would be for me
to make a mountain, a grasshopper, or a lemon. It was no
trouble for You—You're so creative. It's wonderful to have
a friend like You. Help me use my mind to remember
how awesome You've always been. Amen.*

BECOMING A HERO

O **Name two things you think caused Adam to be filled with wonder.**

O **How does worship lead to being a hero of wonder?**

O **Name five things God made that you really like.**

O **When was the last time you thanked God for these things?**

O **What is the opposite of wonder?**

The Best for Me
Noah's Heroic Story
GENESIS 6–9

2

*We can be sure that
we know him if we obey
his commandments.*

1 JOHN 2:3 NLT

God asked Noah to build a very big boat. It would take many years to finish the hard work. People would make fun of Noah.

It would have been easy for Noah to think this was a bad idea. The boat would be built in a place where there was little water. How would it float? The boat was unlike any other boat ever made. Who would use it? Noah would spend so much time building the boat. Who would take care of his family?

But Noah obeyed. Day after day and year after year, Noah worked hard. When the time was right, he learned why God said to build a boat. The largest flood ever known covered the earth. Noah obeyed, and his family was rescued.

Noah was a hero of obedience. He didn't need to know the answer to every question to obey. God had given Noah a job—and Noah went to work.

Sometimes when you're told there's work to do, you can think it's not really important. You wonder if it's fair. You believe someone else should do the job. You wish you didn't have to work.

If God asked you to do a job, you might think you'd be like Noah. You probably think you'd do it. After all, it's God asking, right? But God has already asked you to do some pretty big jobs. He asks you to obey your parents, tell the truth, don't take things that aren't yours, and be happy with what you already have.

Obedience is hard work. It means you believe God knows more than you do. It means that when you obey, you believe God will take care of you. It means you believe God's plan is better than your plan. Best of all, obeying God shows Him that you love Him.

God said people would disobey Him, but He's never stopped asking for obedience.

Noah was heroic when he obeyed. You can be that kind of hero, too.

God's plans are always better than your questions. His commands always have a reason even when you want to ask, "Why?" God can be trusted, so you can find a way to say yes to His plans by obeying what He asks. Noah obeyed and saved his family. When you obey you're telling God you want the future He has in mind for you.

Dear God, sometimes I wonder why You gave me rules
to follow. Sometimes Your rules seem like a punishment,
but if Noah is a hero of obedience and he worked
for years to build Your boat, then maybe I have some
growing up to do. I will probably disobey, but I want
You to help me understand that Your rules are important and
that You have reasons why You want me to do what
You ask. Help me to believe that You always want the best
for me and that Your way is better than mine. Amen.

BECOMING A HERO

- Why was it so important for Noah to obey?

- Why is it so hard to obey?

- Name one thing you were asked to do that you still have time to do today.

- Why do you think obedience is a way to show God how much you love Him?

- What is the opposite of obedience?

3

The Trust Test
Abraham's Heroic Story
GENESIS 22

Do not throw away this confident trust in the Lord. Remember the great reward it brings you!

HEBREWS 10:35 NLT

Abraham loved his son, but God took first place. God gave Abraham a trust test—and Abraham passed the test. He was asked to trust God with the life of his son, Isaac, even if it meant Abraham would never see his son again.

The test wasn't whether God trusted Abraham. The test was whether Abraham trusted God. Abraham did, and trust made him a hero.

God loves you, but do you trust Him? God can forgive you, but do you believe it? God is for you, but do you have faith in that?

He takes care of everything, including you. God made the sun come up this morning, just like it did yesterday. He's always made autumn follow summer. He's made sure that every time you take a breath there will be enough air.

You might think these are small things, but if God can be trusted to make sure these things happen, then what else can you trust Him to do for you?

Trusting someone means you believe they will do what they say, act like they should, and really care about you. This was the kind of trust Abraham had for God. God made sure Abraham had what he needed. With each promise God made and with each promise God kept, Abraham discovered that God could be trusted. So, Abraham trusted.

If God were the power company, you'd never have to worry about a power outage. If God were the water company, you'd never be thirsty. If God were the gas company, you'd never be cold. God is totally dependable, absolutely trustworthy, and keeps every promise He's ever made.

God loved Abraham—and He loves you, too. Learn from Abraham and decide to trust that everything God will ever ask you to do will be helpful, a blessing, and cause you grow to be more like Him.

Even when you make the choice not to trust, God can still be trusted. Romans 8:28 (NLT) says, "We know that God causes everything to work together for the good of those who love God and are called according to his purpose for them."

God can take those times when you don't trust Him and still prove He can be trusted.

When you trust God, you're saying He can be in control, you're willing to obey, and you believe His plan is the best plan you could ever follow.

Dear God, being a hero of trust is hard. You might ask me to give up something I like. You might ask me to do something that seems impossible. Sometimes I don't trust myself because I make mistakes. Trusting You should be easy, but I still wonder if everything will be okay. Keep reminding me that even if everyone else lets me down, You never will. Help me to trust You today. Don't be surprised if I ask again tomorrow. Amen.

BECOMING A HERO

- Why do you think Abraham believed God was worth trusting?

- Why don't you trust everyone?

- How do you feel when someone lets you down?

- What is one way you could choose to trust God today?

- What is the opposite of trust?

Growing Up Determined

Jacob's Heroic Story

GENESIS 32

4

I seek you
with all my heart;
do not let me stray from
your commands.

PSALM 119:10 NIV

Jacob was a hero of determination, but when he was young he was determined for all the wrong reasons. He tricked his brother. He tricked his dad. Why? He was determined to get something he really wanted. He didn't care how he got it—even if it hurt other people. It did.

When he really grew up, he was determined for the best reason—he wanted God's blessing. To be a hero his choices had to change. His tricks had to be left behind. God became important to Jacob, and his family noticed.

Jesus was born a hero in every possible way. Jacob was not a hero of determination until he was an older man. You were not born a hero, but you can become one. Jesus can help.

The heroes in this book didn't start out heroic. They were selfish. They sinned. They wanted their own way. They became heroes when they wanted what God wanted. God made them strong when they understood they needed help. They became courageous when they stopped being afraid.

Heroes are people you look up to because they help others. Jacob is a hero of determination because when he finally made the choice to follow God, he used what he believed in his heart, knew in his mind, and planted in his soul. Then he determined to finish well.

You can start being determined today, too. You can make choices that show God is most important. You can follow God even when others think it's silly. And when you're determined to play sports, win a board game, or ride a bike, remember that these may be accomplishments, but they won't make you a hero. Real determination means you absolutely believe there is nothing more important than following God.

Determination needs to be friends with obedience and cooperation to really grow. God has a plan for you. Being a hero of determination means you will cooperate with God's plan and do what He says.

Whenever you need help, God will help. When you choose to follow God, no matter how hard it can seem, there is a promise in the Bible for you. Philippians 4:13 (NLT) says, "I can do everything through Christ, who gives me strength."

If you are determined to follow God, then He will give you exactly what you need to keep walking in His direction.

Dear God, I don't want to disappoint You. I'm afraid that being a hero of determination will be too hard. You want me to cooperate and obey. Sometimes I don't cooperate or obey, so I know this won't be easy. You promised to help, so I'm asking for help. I want to be more like You, and I want You to make me strong. I believe You are worth following. Please help me be brave enough to follow You. Amen.

• •

BECOMING A HERO

O **Why do you think it was hard for Jacob to be determined?**

O **If you are a hero of determination, how can you cooperate with God's plan when He says, "Obey your parents"?**

O **If you're going to be determined, who can help you the most?**

O **Name one way you can be determined for God today.**

O **What is the opposite of determination?**

5

The Bad Day Collection

Joseph's Heroic Story
GENESIS 37–41

God blesses those who patiently endure testing and temptation.

JAMES 1:12 NLT

Jacob had twelve sons. He loved them all, but Jacob thought his son Joseph was extra special. Because Jacob played favorites, Joseph's brothers were jealous. One day they were so upset with Joseph they sold him as a slave. This wasn't supposed to happen to a special son.

Joseph was taken away from his home. He was sold again in Egypt. He didn't know anyone. Everything was different. He must have been confused and sad, but Joseph was a hero of endurance. This type of hero lives with hard days for a long time. He spends time with unpleasant people and still finds a way to survive.

Joseph met people who called him a liar when he hadn't lied. Joseph met people who said they would help but didn't help. Joseph met people who called him trustworthy, but he was still locked up in prison.

Being a hero of endurance may mean that people will say things about you that aren't true, that you have a large collection of bad days, and that life doesn't seem fair.

There's something about living through hard days that can help you become more like Jesus. God's opinion of you doesn't change. He loves you. He's on your side. He knows the truth. You can endure every hard thing because God's opinion always matters most.

Finish a race and you have endured to the end. Finish a hard test and you have endured to the last question. Believe that when other people say things that aren't true about you, God knows the truth and can help you endure unfair treatment.

If things are really hard, you can talk to your parents or a teacher, but it's always best to talk to God. He has a lot of practice at endurance. He's an expert. Psalm 118:1 (NLT) says, "Give thanks to the LORD, for he is good! His faithful love endures forever."

Every human would cause God to have a really bad day if He didn't love them. He made a choice to love you, and He's never gone back on His word. Make a bad choice and He will still love you. God's love is even offered to people who say bad things about Him.

If God has endured unkindness from all the people who have ever lived on earth, then maybe you can endure unkindness from a few. To be a hero of endurance means you exercise your patience and kindness muscles. God can make you stronger.

Dear God, I can't imagine what it's like to have people saying mean things about You all the time. Sometimes I get angry when people are unkind. Help me remember that Your kindness is offered to me every day. Enduring bad days is hard, but it helps knowing I never have to endure alone. Joseph endured a lot and You were with him. Be with me. Help me endure. Amen.

BECOMING A HERO

O **Name two things Joseph had to endure.**

O **Name two things you have to endure.**

O **Why do you think it is so hard to endure when people are mean?**

O **Name someone you know who is a good example of endurance.**

O **What is the opposite of endurance?**

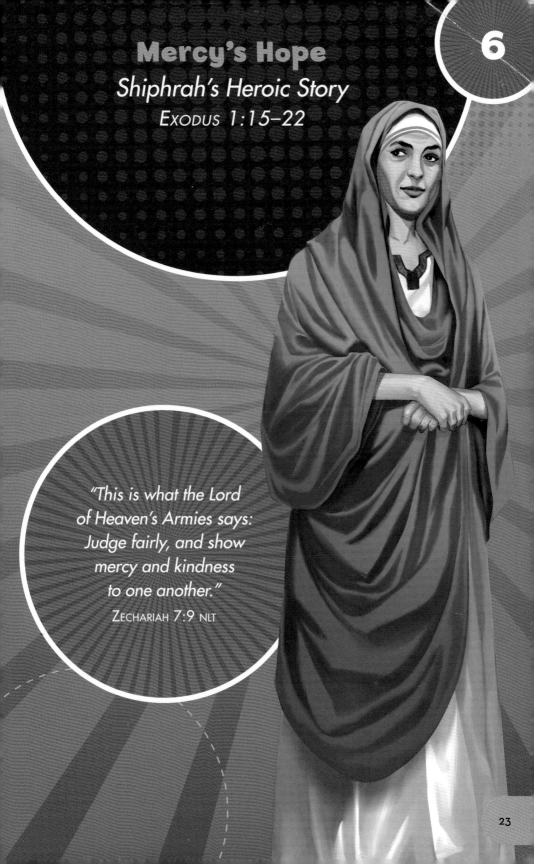

6

Mercy's Hope
Shiphrah's Heroic Story
Exodus 1:15–22

"This is what the Lord of Heaven's Armies says: Judge fairly, and show mercy and kindness to one another."

Zechariah 7:9 NLT

Shiphrah wasn't a doctor, but people always needed her help. She was called a midwife, and she helped mothers when they were going to have babies. She was good at her job. She loved God. She became a hero.

Moses was a man God used to help rescue His people. Just before he was born, the king told Shiphrah that any baby boy born to Moses' family was to be killed. Shiphrah knew God did not want people to kill other people. She knew she couldn't do this wicked thing.

She kept her appointments. Shiphrah helped Moses' mother through the birth of her son, and the boy lived. Many boys in his family lived. The king felt threatened. The king was not happy. The king did not understand the kindness of mercy.

Shiphrah gave something to Moses that the king wouldn't. She was merciful. She saved the lives of many boys in a time when one king thought a bad law was good.

Mercy treats others better than they thought they deserved. Mercy refuses to punish when someone does something wrong. Mercy is a kindness that's given even when others can't pay it back yet. Mercy is a heroic companion to love and grace.

Luke 6:36 (NIV) says, "Be merciful, just as your Father is merciful." Matthew 5:7 (NLT) says, "God blesses those who are merciful, for they will be shown mercy." God is the teacher of mercy. It was His good idea. He promises mercy to those who show mercy. He doesn't want you to get even. He wants you to show mercy. It's what He did for you. He is your example.

Justice tells others, "See, I told you so." Mercy says, "It looks like you've had a bad day." Justice says, "You're getting what you deserve." Mercy says, "How can I help?"

Mercy cares mainly about people. Justice cares most about making everything fair. Justice is important, but mercy is a gift of love.

Shiphrah knew the king's rule wasn't fair. She knew the rule didn't match God's plan. She couldn't change the king's mind, but she could show mercy to Moses. She wanted God to be pleased. She obeyed God. She became a hero of mercy. Today Shiphrah is remembered.

Dear God, You are the only One who always makes the right choices. You show justice when You need to, but You love to show mercy to people who need it. Help me learn to love people so I can also show mercy. Everyone does things You've said not to do. If You didn't show mercy, things would be very hard. Because You forgive, help me to forgive. Because You love, help me love. Because You show mercy, help me to show mercy. Amen.

BECOMING A HERO

○ **Why do you think mercy was important to Shiphrah?**

○ **How would you describe mercy?**

○ **Why do you think God said mercy is so important?**

○ **Do you ever feel like getting even with someone? What did you learn from Shiphrah's story that helped?**

○ **What is the opposite of mercy?**

7

She Showed Respect

Jochebed's Heroic Story

Exodus 2:1–11

Love each other with genuine affection, and take delight in honoring each other.

Romans 12:10 nlt

Jochebed was about to have a baby. When she wondered what the baby would look like, she was happy. When she wondered if the baby was a boy, she was sad. She already had a daughter and a son, but the king thought baby boys were his enemies. Jochebed couldn't face her problem alone.

It wouldn't be long before Shiphrah came to Jochebed's house to help deliver the baby. That's when the problems for Jochebed began.

The king's bad law said that the midwife was supposed to kill all baby boys. When Jochebed heard Moses cry for the first time she cried with him, but Shiphrah did not kill Moses. Jochebed's tears turned to joy.

It wasn't long before the wicked king changed the law again. All newborn baby boys must die, even if they were a few months old. Jochebed hid baby Moses because she agreed with God—all life is important and should be respected.

Jochebed wanted to protect her new son from harm. Her respect for the life of baby Moses meant she would pray to God and then do what she could to keep him safe.

You show respect to God every time you do what He asks you to do. You can start by loving God, obeying your parents, and telling the truth. Like Jochebed, you will make choices that seem hard, but God asks you to respect His commands, and He will always bless obedience.

God's rules should be important to you because they're important to God. The reason for the rules is to help you learn how to really love others. When you love others, you won't want to hurt them and you won't try to take something from them, but you *will* want to do what's best for them.

This is what God does for you. He is your example. You show respect when you learn to love. You can love others because God loved you first. God never asks you to do something that doesn't help other people. You honor God every time you make right choices. It means you're growing up. It means you're standing up. It means that when you need help you can look up, and God will help.

Jochebed respected God, life, and a future for her son, Moses. Her name may be new to you, but hopefully you can learn something wonderful about respect from this great Bible hero.

Dear God, I want to show respect to You. Help me remember that when I respect Your rules I'm showing You respect. I can show respect at school by obeying classroom rules. I can show respect at my friend's house by honoring the authority of their parents. I can show respect to my parents by learning what they want me to do and doing it without even being asked. I learned this from You. Thanks. Amen.

BECOMING A HERO

O **How did Jochebed show respect?**

O **Why do you think respect is so important?**

O **How can love make respect stronger?**

O **Why do you think obedience is part of respecting God?**

O **What is the opposite of respect?**

8

Follow His Lead

Moses' Heroic Story

Exodus 2–20

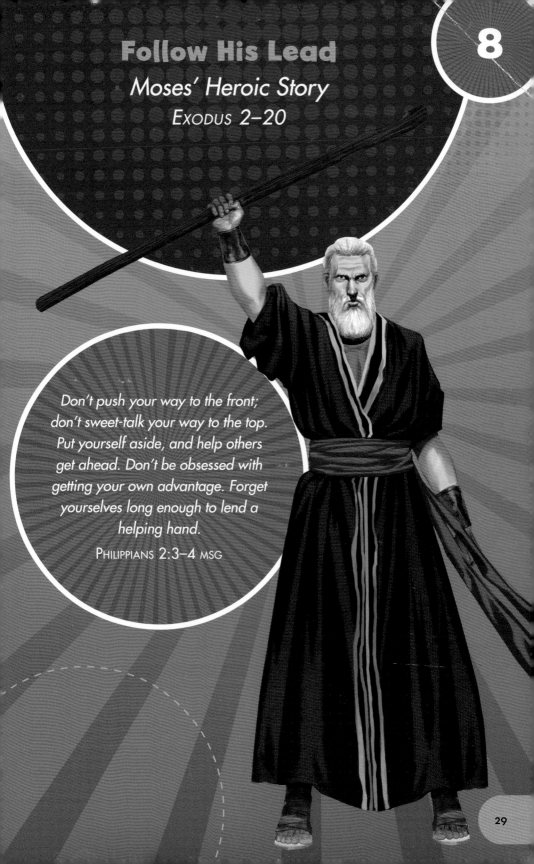

Don't push your way to the front; don't sweet-talk your way to the top. Put yourself aside, and help others get ahead. Don't be obsessed with getting your own advantage. Forget yourselves long enough to lend a helping hand.

PHILIPPIANS 2:3–4 MSG

Moses never stayed in one place for very long. He moved a lot. For many years he lived in the wilderness where there were more sheep than people. Moses spent a lot of time by himself.

One day God gave him the job of being a leader. God wanted Moses to rescue His people from slavery. Moses tried to argue. He told God he didn't even know how to speak the right words. He wanted to give up before he ever started his new job. The only leadership Moses had ever been good at was moving sheep from one meadow to another. Besides, he was eighty years old. He wasn't sure anyone would follow him.

God sent Moses to Egypt to rescue His family. God gave him directions. God gave him the right words. God gave him the strength to lead the people through the desert to a home that God promised to give them.

God can take people you'd never expect and give them a job you wouldn't think they could do.

Leaders help others win. Leaders walk with people who follow and help them reach the end of the race. Good leaders don't boss people around; they get things done by showing how to do what needs to be done. Leaders don't expect others to know it all, and they're willing to be kind teachers.

Moses was a leader who proved he could be trusted. God used Moses because he wasn't a know-it-all. Moses kept coming back to God for help.

Being a hero of leadership doesn't mean giving people orders while you watch them work. God could use Moses because he was even more interested in following God than leading the people. Sometimes God chooses people to lead because they are willing to follow directions.

God might call you to be a leader. When He does, you should always remember He loves the people you lead. Since people matter to God, they should matter to you. There's no need to try to prove you're better, stronger, smarter, or more popular. If you lead, you should look for ways to help those who follow.

Moses learned to be a hero of leadership by following the God who takes ordinary people and gives them the chance to do something amazing. For Moses that was leading more than a million people to their new home. Ask God to help you learn what He wants you to do. He will.

Dear God, thank You for helping me understand that good leaders are great followers. They just have to remember to follow You. I don't know what You have planned for my future, but I want to follow You even if I'm never considered a leader. Help me love You enough to be kind to people You've created. May my example be something other people can follow. Amen.

• •

BECOMING A HERO

O **What made Moses such a good leader?**

O **What was your favorite part of Moses' story? Why?**

O **Why do you think it is so important for leaders to follow God?**

O **How is leadership different than being bossy?**

O **What is the opposite of leadership?**

9

A Fearless Report

Caleb's Heroic Story

NUMBERS 13–14

Be on guard.
Stand firm in the faith.
Be courageous. Be strong.
1 CORINTHIANS 16:13 NLT

Moses led the people *away* from Egypt and *toward* the land God had promised to give them. The people were excited to have a place they could really call home. Twelve men were picked to walk through the new land. Then they came back to tell the people about their adventures.

Caleb was one of the men. For forty days he was filled with wonder. This land was perfect. Grapes grew so big two men had to carry one cluster. This land could provide for the people, and Caleb was ready to put out a welcome mat and enjoy God's gift of a new home.

Imagine how surprised Caleb was when most of the other men who explored the land told the people they were too weak to take the land. They said it was impossible.

Caleb must have thought, *Are they saying God is too small to keep His promise?* But Caleb had fearless faith. He knew that if God gave them the land, they just needed to call it home.

Ten men out of twelve didn't believe God could do the impossible. God told Moses, "Because your men explored the land for forty days, you must wander in the wilderness for forty years—a year for each day, suffering the consequences of your sins" (Numbers 14:34 NLT).

Caleb must have found it hard to believe the people would give up the home God had for them and wander in the wilderness for forty years. It didn't make sense. God had noticed Caleb's fearless faith and promised him that he would live to have a home in the beautiful land he had explored.

God's plan for your life is so much bigger, better, and more wonderful than any plans you could think up. God might let you have your way, but you could be missing out on a most exciting surprise.

When you let fear live inside, it will always try to push faith out the door. Isaiah 41:10 (NLT) says, "Don't be afraid, for I am with you. Don't be discouraged, for I am your God. I will strengthen you and help you. I will hold you up with my victorious right hand."

The way you respond to God is important. He wants you to trust that He knows what He's doing. He wants you to believe His plans are the best. He wants you to take all your faith and give it to Him. Then you can tell fear it's no longer welcome. Caleb was the hero of fearless faith, and God gave him a home. God keeps His promises.

*Dear God, I don't like being afraid, and there are lots of
things that frighten me, but I never want to let my fears keep
me from following Your good plans. I want to trust You.
I want to believe Your plan is best. I want to obey and
watch Your promises come true. Amen.*

BECOMING A HERO

○ **Why do you think Caleb is considered a fearless hero?**

○ **What makes you afraid?**

○ **Why does it help knowing that God has a plan for your future?**

○ **What have you learned that can turn your fear into fearless faith?**

○ **What is the opposite of being fearless?**

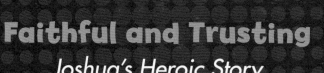

Faithful and Trusting

Joshua's Heroic Story
JOSHUA 6, 24

10

A person who is put in charge as a manager must be faithful.

1 CORINTHIANS 4:2 NLT

Joshua heard about Moses. He was the man who would deliver Israel from Egypt. Joshua was much younger than Moses, but the two men became good friends. Moses trusted Joshua and taught him well. Joshua trusted Moses and was faithful to God.

It wasn't long after Joshua met Moses that he was given a big job. He was one of twelve men sent to explore the land God said would be their new home, but forty years had passed since Joshua first walked through the promised land. The people spent years wandering in the desert. They were tired of living in tents. They were tired of walking. They just wanted a place to call home.

When Moses could no longer lead the people, God chose Joshua to show the people the way home. Joshua remembered God had given the people a good place to live. Time was a good teacher. The people finally trusted God enough to accept His gift. Joshua was pleased.

Every time God told Joshua what to do, Joshua followed instructions. Every difficult job was completed because God gave Joshua strength. Every step forward was a new gift from a good God.

Joshua wasn't put in charge just because he was a friend of Moses. He didn't get the job because people liked him the best. He wasn't the one to lead Israel because he won a prize for being bossier than anyone else. Joshua was picked to lead the people because He trusted God and was faithful to do what God asked.

God has always looked for faithful men, women, boys, and girls to follow Him. He's looking for people who trust His plan and follow instructions. Because He is totally faithful to you, He's looking to see if you will be faithful to Him.

Faithfulness to God means trusting His plan. Faithfulness to God means that what He thinks is more important than what anyone else thinks. Faithfulness to God means following where He leads even when the way seems hard. Faithfulness means standing up for what is right even when most people choose what is wrong.

Joshua was faithful even after waiting forty years to finally have a place to call home. He could have given up, but he didn't. He could have said, "What's the use?" but he remembered a promise God made to more than a million people. He could have followed his own plan, but God's plan was better.

Joshua believed, refused to give up, and God brought him home.

Dear God, I want to be faithful to You. I want to want what You want. I need to believe that Your way is better than mine. It is good to read about Joshua, the hero of faithfulness. He believed Your promise could be trusted for forty years. He lived to see Your promise come true. Joshua's faithfulness matched Your plan. You are worth following. Help me follow. Amen.

• •

BECOMING A HERO

○ **Why do you think it was important that Joshua was faithful to God's plan for so long?**

○ **Why do you think God wants faithful followers?**

○ **Why do you think it's so easy to give up when things get hard?**

○ **Has anyone been faithful to you? How did it make you feel?**

○ **What is the opposite of faithfulness?**

11

The Jar and Horn Soldier

Gideon's Heroic Story
JUDGES 7

Soldiers don't get tied up in the affairs of civilian life, for then they cannot please the officer who enlisted them.

2 TIMOTHY 2:4 NLT

A soldier is trained. A soldier follows commands. A soldier has a hard job.

Gideon was a good soldier. God gave him a command to fight against the people of Midian. For seven years Midian had made life difficult for God's people. Gideon told the people there would be a war.

It wasn't long before thirty-two thousand men showed up to fight. God was the Commander, so Gideon listened when God said there were too many people. After those who were scared went home, there were ten thousand men left. God said there were still too many men. This must have sounded strange to Gideon because Midian had many more soldiers who were willing to fight.

When it was time to stand up to Midian, Gideon was left with just three hundred men. God knew this was more than enough. Three hundred soldiers against thousands of Midianites? It didn't seem fair. Before the men could complain, Gideon gave them weapons. They must have been confused when they were given something they would never think of using to win a battle—clay jars and horns.

The men hid in the hills. From where they hid they could see the Midianite soldiers in the valley below. When the small group of soldiers received the signal, they broke their jars, blew their horns, and shouted, "For the LORD and for Gideon!"

The Midianite soldiers were so confused they started fighting each other and ran away in fear.

Gideon is a hero because he was a solider. Most people wouldn't have believed what Gideon did was possible. But it was God's plan. Gideon obeyed his Commander.

A soldier isn't just a warrior. A soldier is an obedient follower. When God gave the command, Gideon believed the Commander knew what He was doing.

You can be a heroic soldier for God, too. Start by obeying the things He has already commanded. Love people, share what you have, and be kind.

You might think you don't have the right tools to do the job. That's when you need to remember Gideon's soldiers. They fought with weapons most people wouldn't think to use. In the hands of soldiers who follow

God's directions, they won a war using clay and air made by God.

Fight hate with love. Fight selfishness with kindness. Fight greed with giving.

God's soldiers are obedient heroes.

*Dear God, being a soldier seems like hard work.
It seems like it would be dangerous to be a soldier.
Gideon was a hero because he chose to follow You. If You
want me to be a soldier, would You help me obey Your
commands? Would You help me see that the way You win
is different than the way I expect? Help me understand
that You have a plan—and it's good. Amen.*

· ·

BECOMING A HERO

O **Why do you think so many soldiers were scared?**

O **How do you think the 300 soldiers felt when they received a clay jar and a horn?**

O **How has the way you think about God's soldiers changed after reading today's story?**

O **How can you become a hero like Gideon?**

O **What might cause this hero to become weak?**

12

The Strong Became Weak

Samson's Heroic Story

JUDGES 13–16

*Be strong in the Lord
and in his mighty power.*

EPHESIANS 6:10 NLT

Samson was strong because God made him strong. Samson was strong *as long* as he obeyed God. Samson was the hero of strength, but this hero made a mistake.

Samson had defeated many enemies. If there had been any *strong man* competitions, he would have won—every time. He tore gates from city walls and carried them miles away. People tried to capture Samson. Every time they tried, they failed.

That was before Samson met Delilah. He thought she was beautiful. She just wanted to know what made him so strong. What Delilah didn't know was that God had decided to use Samson. God promised Samson would stay strong as long as he didn't cut his hair. Samson's long hair was his way of showing he belonged to God.

Delilah kept asking Samson to tell her what made him strong, but he wouldn't give her the answer. *He was strong because God made him strong.*

One day Samson finally told Delilah what made him strong. When he fell asleep, the hair he had grown since birth was cut off. The hero of strength became weak.

In 2 Corinthians 12:9–10 (NLT) when God told Paul, "My grace is all you need. My power works best in weakness," Paul responded, "I am glad to boast about my weaknesses, so that the power of Christ can work through me. . . . For when I am weak, then I am strong."

You are strong because God makes you strong. When you're weak God can give you all the strength you need. Samson had strong muscles. Your strength might be in making good choices, caring for others, or helping when people need help.

You can be a hero of strength when you remember who gave you strength. He's the God who gave Samson strength. This hero failed when he thought he could do everything on his own. He stopped looking to God for help. When he didn't have God's help, Samson became weak.

God made it very clear to Samson and He makes it very clear to you that His strength is what makes a difference. Whenever you try to do things without His help, you will always struggle.

Think about this verse in 1 Corinthians 1:27 (NLT): "God chose things the world considers foolish in order to shame those who think they are wise. And he chose things that are powerless to shame those who are powerful."

God wants to make you strong, but you have to accept His strength.

Dear God, You want to make me strong. You want Your strength to be mine. Why do I always want to try to do things on my own? I think I can understand Samson. He wanted to use his strength to impress people. When he didn't think about You, he became weak. Help me remember to ask for Your help. Help me always to use Your strength. Amen.

• •

BECOMING A HERO

○ **Why do you think Samson turned his strength into a reason to be proud?**

○ **Why do you think God had to remind Samson where his strength came from?**

○ **When did Samson stop being the hero of strength?**

○ **When was the last time you asked God to give you strength?**

○ **What is the opposite of strength?**

The Hard Choice
Ruth's Heroic Story
THE BOOK OF RUTH

When she speaks she has
something worthwhile to say,
and she always says it kindly.

PROVERBS 31:26 MSG

ou might be asked to do something hard. You might be asked to do something you don't want to do. You might want to say, "No!"

What if you made a choice to do a hard thing without even being asked? What if this hard thing was the right thing to do? What if it changed your life?

Ruth considered these questions, and a few more. Her husband had died. Her brother-in-law had died. Her father-in-law had died. Ruth was sad. Her mother-in-law, Naomi, was angry.

Naomi decided it was time to leave Moab and return to her hometown in Bethlehem. Ruth had always lived in Moab. Ruth made a very hard choice before Naomi planned to leave. Ruth would go with her mother-in-law. Ruth's choice meant she would leave her parents. She would leave her friends. She had no idea how hard things would be. Ruth was kind, and it showed up in her choice to follow Naomi to Bethlehem. Ruth became a hero of compassion.

There was no job for her in Bethlehem. Ruth and Naomi would have to do whatever they could just to live. Ruth picked the harvested grain for whatever was left over. It was hard work, but Ruth came back with enough to feed herself and her mother-in-law.

Her friends might have said living in Moab would have been better. She would have had enough food. She wouldn't have had to work so hard every day. She might have had an easier life.

But if Ruth had stayed in Moab, so many stories would be different. You see, Ruth married Boaz, a relative of Naomi. Ruth would become the grandmother of King David. Ruth helped Naomi, and Naomi's anger went away. God had a plan, and Ruth said, "Yes!" When Jesus was born, Ruth was listed as one of His relatives. Ruth was a part of the story of Jesus.

When you have to make hard decisions. . .when you know what's right but struggle with doing the right thing. . .and when there are easier choices you could make, remember it was compassion that caused a young woman named Ruth to do the hardest thing she had ever done—for all the right reasons.

The kindness and compassion Ruth had for Naomi made it possible for God to give her great honor and a better purpose.

When you let God give you directions, you allow Jesus to be part of *your* story.

Remember, compassion loves people, and kindness finds ways to help.

Dear God, help me to see compassion is the right choice. Help me show kindness because You are kind. In every hard choice, help me recognize that You can be trusted to walk with me when I don't understand. You always give more than I can. You love more than I will. Your compassion is fresh every morning. Thank You. Amen.

• •

BECOMING A HERO

○ **Why do you think it would be hard to make a choice like Ruth's?**

○ **What is the hardest choice you've ever had to make?**

○ **Are you happy with the choice you made? Why?**

○ **Why do you think it's hard to always make the right choice?**

○ **What is the opposite of compassion?**

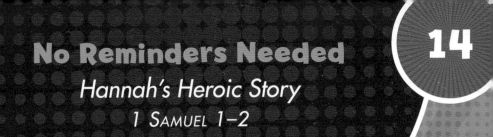

Seek the Kingdom of God above all else, and live righteously, and he will give you everything you need.

MATTHEW 6:33 NLT

nitiative is a big word. It means being able to decide what needs to be done and then doing it without anyone telling you to do it.

You could show initiative by seeing that the garbage needs to be emptied and emptying it without a reminder. You could remember to make your bed without someone telling you to make your bed. You could help with the dishes even if it's not your regular job.

Hannah is a hero of initiative. She had been married for several years. She did not have any children. Hannah really wanted children. She went to the temple and prayed for a son. Hannah knew God had all the power to answer her prayer. If anyone could help Hannah, it was God.

But Hannah did something no one expected. She offered to give her son to God even before she knew whether God would answer her prayer. God said yes to her prayer. Hannah was very happy.

When her son was old enough, Hannah took Samuel to the temple where he lived and worked with the priest, Eli.

God used Hannah's initiative to show what it looks like to be selfless. Hannah cared more about honoring the promise she made to God than trying to make a new deal she liked better with God. When Hannah said she would offer Samuel as a thank-you gift to God, she meant it.

Hannah had more children after Samuel went to live in the temple, but both mother and son would remember that God gave the gift of life. They both believed that seeking God was the best first choice. Both sought God's plan—and found answers.

If initiative is being able to decide what needs to be done and then doing it without anyone telling you to do it, then you show initiative every time you pray to God without being reminded. Like Hannah, you're learning that God has answers to the hardest questions. He has a plan, and He's been waiting for you to be interested enough to ask Him to show you.

Initiative is seeking to know, love, and serve God without anyone telling you. Initiative is reading God's words in the Bible without being reminded that it's a good idea. It's what heroes—just like you—do.

Dear God, sometimes I wonder why it is so easy to let other people remind me of what I need to do. It could be chores, homework, or saying thanks. You want me to have the initiative to pray to You and read the Bible without being reminded. Maybe it just shows I love You enough to keep in touch. Maybe it shows that I love You and respect Your plans for me. Amen.

● ●

BECOMING A HERO

O **According to the verse at the beginning of this reading what are you supposed to do?**

O **How did Hannah seek God's kingdom first?**

O **Is it harder to follow a command or do the right thing without being told? Why?**

O **What is one way you can show initiative today?**

O **What is the opposite of initiative?**

15

Available and Listening

Samuel's Heroic Story

1 Samuel 3, 7, 16

God has given each of you a gift from his great variety of spiritual gifts. Use them well to serve one another.

1 Peter 4:10 NLT

It's been said that God cares more about availability than experience. That means if you're available for God to use, then He will use you. If you wait until you think you know everything, then you probably aren't learning from God.

Samuel was young when his mother, Hannah, brought him to live in the temple and work with the priest Eli.

Eli had learned so much about God. He had many teachers. He had taken many tests. People looked to Eli for guidance. But God didn't come to talk to Eli. He came to talk to young Samuel. Maybe Eli was sad when he heard the news, but the old priest told Samuel to listen to God's voice.

As Samuel grew, God asked him to find the first two kings of his people, Saul and David. God asked him to tell the people what He said. People paid attention to Samuel.

Sometimes God asked Samuel to tell the people things they didn't want to hear. Samuel spoke the words. Why did God use Samuel? Because he was available. He was willing.

God has always used ordinary people to do big things. Ordinary people find it easy to give God credit for the amazing things He does. They honor God with their obedience.

Letting God teach you through the words of the Bible and the encouragement of other Christians is a great way to show you're available for God to use. He's always looking for boys and girls who are willing to follow. He allowed the young boy Samuel to teach the priest Eli. He allowed a young man named Timothy to become a preacher at one of the first churches. Jesus invited children to come and see Him when he visited. God loves children. He wants them to be part of His plan. He wants them to be *available*.

Being available to God means you can think of nothing more important than doing what God wants. It means you're willing to change your plans for God's plans. It means you will follow God even when it's not easy.

When you make yourself available to God, you will be able to help others, discover joy, and let God lead you to adventure. God offers many good gifts to those who are available.

Dear God, I want to be available for You to use, but sometimes I'm afraid that You might ask me to do something that's really hard. Help me to remember that You are always with me and can help me when I don't know what to do. Help me to remember that I can call on You anytime. You never ask me to do anything alone. Help me to understand that when I make myself available, I shouldn't be surprised when You give me something important to do. Amen.

• •

BECOMING A HERO

O **How do you think Eli felt knowing God was talking to a young boy?**

O **Why do you think God chose to talk to Samuel instead of the priest Eli?**

O **Why do you think God uses people who are willing to help?**

O **How can you make yourself available to God today?**

O **What is the opposite of being available?**

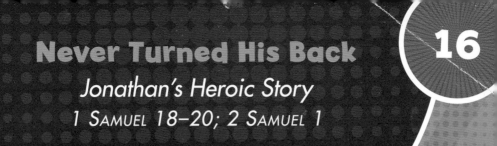

Never Turned His Back

Jonathan's Heroic Story
1 Samuel 18–20; 2 Samuel 1

16

Friends come and friends go, but a true friend sticks by you like family.
PROVERBS 18:24 MSG

Everyone wants at least one good friend. Sometimes someone can be friendly but never actually become a friend. Sometimes people who have been friends stop being friends. Sometimes you might find friendship that will last the rest of your life.

David was a boy who grew up to become king. When he was young, he took care of sheep. Sheep were nice in their own way, but they weren't really friends. They were animals.

Jonathan was King Saul's son. People treated him like he was very special. People were friendly to him, but they weren't really friends. They just wanted to impress the king's son.

As a young man, David took a slingshot and fought a giant named Goliath who had been a bully to the army of his country. God helped David win. It didn't take long for the shepherd David to meet Jonathan, son of the king. The two became great friends. Jonathan wasn't a sheep. David didn't try to impress Jonathan.

Jonathan helped David. David helped Jonathan. King Saul became jealous and tried to hurt David, but Jonathan protected his friend. Jonathan was a trustworthy hero. He didn't let people decide whether he could be friends with David. He didn't try to impress people by pretending he didn't like David. Jonathan never stopped being David's friend. David never forgot Jonathan's friendship.

You can and should be a trustworthy friend. You can and should be a trustworthy student. You can and should be a trustworthy child. Being trustworthy makes you a hero.

People like to find someone who will be trustworthy, who will do what they say they will do, and who will be there when they are needed. Maybe you are that *someone*.

Jonathan is a trustworthy hero because he treated David very much like God treats you. God protects, cares, and helps without taking a poll to see if other people think you're worth the effort. God doesn't wait to see who's going to be the most popular and then try to impress them with His *God gifts*.

Whenever you need a friend, you should remember that God has been looking for a friend just like you. Unlike some friends, God never leaves you, never turns His back, and never pretends that He doesn't know who you are.

Being trustworthy means you share time, life, and friendship. Jonathan did that for David. God does that for you. You can do that for someone else.

Being trustworthy is an opportunity to grow up. All good heroes do that.

Dear God, I want trustworthy friends. I want to be a trustworthy friend. I'm grateful You show me every day what it means to be trustworthy. Help me to be friendly, dependable, and someone people can talk to. Keep gossip from my lips, dishonesty from my friendships, and a lack of dependability from my choices. Help me treat my friends the way I want my friends to treat me. Amen.

• •

BECOMING A HERO

○ **What made Jonathan a trustworthy hero?**

○ **Why do you think Jonathan's friendship meant so much to David?**

○ **What traits make for a good friend?**

○ **What's one way you could show trustworthiness to others?**

○ **What is the opposite of being trustworthy?**

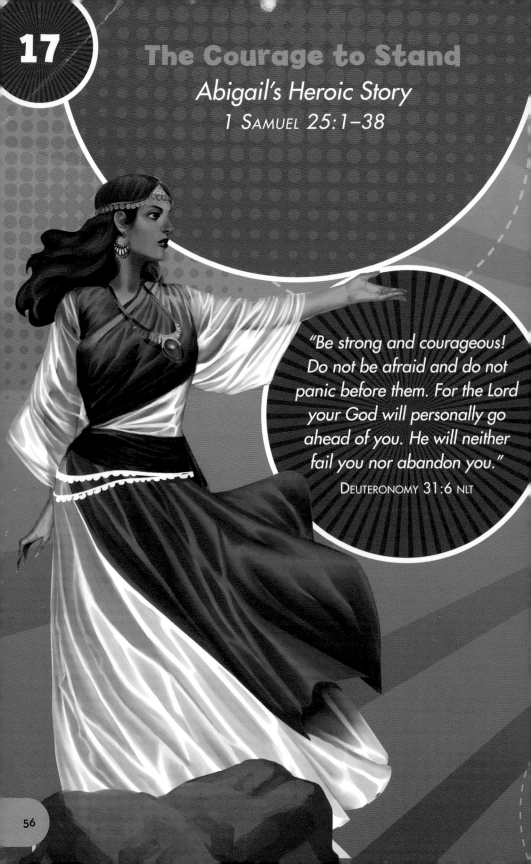

17

The Courage to Stand

Abigail's Heroic Story

1 Samuel 25:1–38

"Be strong and courageous! Do not be afraid and do not panic before them. For the Lord your God will personally go ahead of you. He will neither fail you nor abandon you."

Deuteronomy 31:6 NLT

No matter how hard Jonathan tried, he could not stop his father, King Saul, from chasing his best friend across the country. David had hidden, run for his life, and asked for help. The king didn't care that the prophet Samuel had said David would be the next king. Saul wanted David to go away. Saul didn't want what God wanted.

One day David was traveling with friends. None of the men had eaten much. Everyone was hungry. David saw shepherds in the distance and went to see if they could share any food they might have. The shepherds knew David was a kind man, and they wanted to help, but the sheep belonged to a man named Nabal. Nabal refused to help David. Nabal called David an outlaw. Nabal told David to find his own food. David had never treated Nabal this way. David had been kind and friendly.

Four hundred men who were with David wanted to teach Nabal a lesson. He needed to know that he had been rude to the future king. Nabal had not been kind.

The shepherds who worked for Nabal were scared. David had often helped them when they took the sheep to the wilderness. Nabal's wife, Abigail, was scared. She knew David had protected her husband's land and sheep.

Somehow Abigail found the courage needed to meet David and apologized to the future king. Abigail brought gifts and food. Abigail's courage made it possible for the war between David and her husband, Nabal, to stop before it got started.

Courage sometimes means apologizing for someone else. Courage sometimes looks like kindness when it would be easier to be mean. Courage is a choice to be brave even when you're scared.

Abigail is a hero of courage. She did the hard thing by seeking out the angry future king and apologizing. She saw what needed to be done and didn't let fear stop her from a good choice. She didn't care what others thought. She had the courage to choose peace.

Courage isn't being tough. Courage is being afraid to do something good but doing it anyway. Courage stands strong while others sit in fear. Courage means admitting when you're wrong and asking others to do the same. Courage is heroic.

Dear God, why does it seem so hard to stand up for what's right? Why am I so afraid of what other people will think? Why do I try to impress people who aren't You? Help me to remember that Your truth is more important than the opinions I hear every day. Help me to remember that You walk with me and will stand with me—even when I think I stand alone. Give me the courage to do the right thing. Amen.

BECOMING A HERO

O   **Why do you think Abigail thought it was important to find courage?**

O   **What do you think caused David to stop the war he planned against Nabal?**

O   **When was the last time you wish you had been more courageous? How would courage have helped?**

O   **Why do you think courage is so important?**

O   **What is the opposite of courage?**

The Shepherd King's Kindness

David's Heroic Story
1 Samuel 17; 2 Samuel 9

> The world of the generous gets larger and larger; the world of the stingy gets smaller and smaller. The one who blesses others is abundantly blessed; those who help others are helped.
>
> Proverbs 11:24–25 MSG

18

David was king, but he never forgot the sheep he took care of or the many times King Saul had chased him. He remembered the day Abigail stopped a war with a kind word and some food. David also remembered his friendship with Jonathan.

One day King Saul and Jonathan both died in the same battle. David became king, but he'd lost his best friend. King David wanted to show kindness to Jonathan's family. David was able to find one of Jonathan's sons, Mephibosheth. This young man struggled to walk. His legs didn't work the way David's legs worked. He could use some kindness.

As a shepherd, if a sheep couldn't walk, David would have put it on his shoulders and carried it. David would carry the broken sheep from one place to the next. He would make sure it had food and water. He would keep it protected because it couldn't protect itself.

As a king, David needed the reminder that the people of his kingdom would be looking to him to lead them. He would need the kindness of a shepherd, the strength of a bear, and trust in an awesome God to help lead the people in the direction God had for them.

As a man who followed God, David needed reminders that there were plenty of times God had carried him through bad days and terrible choices.

Taking care of Mephibosheth would remind Kind David that kindness was a gift God gave to mankind and a gift God wants His people to give to others.

Kindness isn't just something you offer to someone who's been kind to you. Kindness is something God wants you to give to people who aren't kind. Kindness is something you offer to people who don't deserve it. Kindness is a gift that expects nothing in return. That makes sense when you remember that *love* is kind. Like love, kindness never needs to be returned to be given.

Mephibosheth had no reason to expect the king would be kind to him. His grandfather, Saul, was not kind to David, so Mephibosheth may have thought he would be in trouble with the king. But David took care of him, ate with him, and helped him in any way he could.

David is a hero of kindness. He showed that kindness can do something wars never can. Kindness turns strangers into friends.

Dear God, there are times when I don't want to be kind. There are moments when I think someone needs to apologize to me before I can be kind. There are times when kindness seems too kind for people who've hurt me. But You were kind. King David was kind. Help me to be kind. Amen.

• •

BECOMING A HERO

○ Can you name a reason why David might have been kind to Mephibosheth?

○ How did being a shepherd first help David to be kind as the king?

○ What makes it so hard to be kind to others?

○ What did you like most about this story of King David?

○ What is the opposite of kindness?

19

A Story of Truth

Nathan's Heroic Story

2 SAMUEL 12:1–24

Teach me your ways, O Lord, that I may live according to your truth! Grant me purity of heart, so that I may honor you.

PSALM 86:11 NLT

A prophet was like a mail carrier from God. Unlike a normal mail carrier, the prophet knew the message that was being sent. It wasn't sealed in an envelope. The message wasn't on paper. The message was in the heart of the prophet, and the prophet spoke the message for all to hear. Nathan was this kind of prophet.

Nathan may not have been eager to share the message God gave him. The message could make the king angry. The message wasn't happy news. The message reminded King David he had sinned.

The king welcomed Nathan. Nathan spoke to the king as if he were a master storyteller. It might have sounded like this: "O King, there is a terrible sin that has happened in our country. A rich farmer had an important guest come to his home. This farmer had plenty of cows and sheep. He could have had his servants take one of them and prepare a feast for his guests. But there was also a poor farmer who only had one sheep. The poor farmer treated the animal as if it were a part of the family. He wouldn't think of making a meal of his friendly lamb."

King David had once been a shepherd, and he found himself very interested in the story. "What happened then?" the king may have asked.

"This is where the rich farmer broke God's rules. He took the small lamb he didn't own from the poor farmer. He fed the lamb to his guest," Nathan said sadly.

King David was very angry. He wanted to know the name of the man who had taken from a poor man when he already had everything he needed. The king wanted to punish the man who would do such a thing. Nathan looked at the king and quietly said, "*You* are that man."

The king had not taken a lamb, but he had taken something that didn't belong to him. Nathan's message was delivered in a way David understood.

David is remembered for seeking forgiveness from God. Nathan is remembered for being a hero of truth. God's message spoken by Nathan meant a king would be restored, a people would have a better example to follow, and the king would always be reminded that God's rules meant something.

A lying prophet was no prophet at all. Nathan understood that the only message God would allow him to speak was truth. When you speak to others about God, speak truth—always.

Dear God, Nathan knew that he couldn't change Your truth just because he was giving Your message to the king. He wanted to honor You more than he wanted to impress King David. Help me to remember that even when truth is hard, it is always the right choice. Speaking truth to others always honors You. Amen.

· ·

BECOMING A HERO

O **Why do you think Nathan's story meant so much to King David?**

O **How do you think the king felt when he realized the story was about him?**

O **How do you feel when someone suggests you may not be telling the truth?**

O **Why is truth so important to God?**

O **What is the opposite of truth?**

Just Ask

Solomon's Heroic Story

1 KINGS 3:1–15

20

> If you don't know what you're doing, pray to the Father. He loves to help.
>
> JAMES 1:5 MSG

65

When God gives you a job, He also gives you a gift. When He gives you the job of loving others, He loves you first so you know how to love. When the job is forgiving others, He forgives you first so you know what it feels like to be forgiven. When the job God gives you is kindness, you can be sure He was kind to you before He gave you the job.

Solomon was one of King David's sons. He was given the big job of being king after his father. He had never been a king before. He had never had so many decisions to make.

God offered a gift to Solomon. The new king could ask for anything he wanted. God said He would make sure Solomon got it. Solomon thought about what he wanted from God. He could have asked for money. He could have asked to live a long time. He could have asked to always win in every war his country fought. He could have. He didn't.

Solomon decided that if he was to be the wise leader his people needed, then the gift he wanted most was wisdom. God thought this was the perfect gift. God gave the gift of wisdom to Solomon, and there has never been a king who was as wise as this king who asked for wisdom over money or a long life or a strong army.

Because Solomon asked for what he needed most, God also gave him many things the new king had not asked for. Solomon was rich. He became very famous. His people lived in peace—not war.

God reminded Solomon that he needed to remember who gave the gifts if he really wanted to follow God. The Gift Giver was the God who led King David. He was the God who had made and *kept* a promise to Abraham. This was the same God who had created the earth and everything in it. No, it would not be wise to forget God.

God gave Solomon the words for the books of Proverbs, Ecclesiastes, and Song of Solomon. He even gave him the words to two of the Psalms.

God will give you a job to do. When you do what He asks, He will give you everything you need to do the job right. When you work for God, He always gives you the tools you need. He gives you the skills. He gives you every reason to serve Him well.

Dear God, it's easy to think that the jobs You give are for people who are grown up. It can be easy to think You couldn't use someone my size. Thanks for reminding me that when You ask, You also make sure I have Your help in getting the job done right. Help me say yes when You give me a job. Help me learn from the work. Help me do the job in a way that pleases You. Amen.

● ●

BECOMING A HERO

O **Why do you think God was pleased with Solomon's request for wisdom?**

O **Why do you think Solomon needed this gift?**

O **Why do you think God wants you to ask Him for wisdom?**

O **Have you ever asked for this gift?**

O **What is the opposite of wisdom?**

21

The Troublemaker God Loved

Elijah's Heroic Story

1 Kings 18

Prophecy resulted when the Holy Spirit prompted men and women to speak God's Word.

2 Peter 1:21 MSG

ou could be a prophet. It's true. A prophet is encouraged by God's Spirit to speak God's words. The biggest difference between you and the prophets in the Bible is that you can speak words that God has already spoken, but the prophets in the Bible spoke new words God sent them to speak to others.

Elijah spoke God's new words. God told him to tell King Ahab that it would not rain, and it didn't rain. King Ahab didn't like the message. King Ahab didn't like the messenger. King Ahab called Elijah a troublemaker.

Elijah's message was an invitation for the wicked king to come back to God's plan for right living. The king refused to listen. He refused to follow God. He searched for more wickedness than anyone would ever need.

It had been more than three years and still no rain, no clouds in the sky, no lightning, and no thunder. The earth became dry, streams stopped flowing, and plants died. The people were hungry, but King Ahab was close friends with wickedness. The land needed help, and so did the king.

One day Elijah told Ahab that God had another message for him. The king met Elijah on Mount Carmel to hear what God had to say. The king brought hundreds of people with him. Elijah was not scared.

Elijah said God wanted the people to follow Him once more, but they acted like they didn't even know God. Everyone wanted to see Elijah, the troublemaker. No one admitted that God was more important than wickedness.

Elijah was a hero. Elijah was a prophet. Elijah showed God's power and proved the weakness of Baal, the false god King Ahab followed. Elijah told the king to return to the palace because rain was coming.

Maybe some of the people laughed. Elijah predicted rain when there had been no rain. Others had seen God's power and Baal's weakness. Maybe they looked up at the skies searching for a cloud.

The rain came. Heavy rain. Thunder. Lightning. Black skies. The people were amazed. Elijah had prayed that there would be no rain, and the rain stopped coming. Elijah prayed for the rain to come, and rain brought life back to the dry land.

It wasn't Elijah who brought the rain. He wasn't a magician with a bag of tricks. Elijah heroically spoke for God, and God sent the rain.

You can be part of the family that shares God's message with others. You can tell people about the love God has for them. You can remind people that God forgives. You can even remind other Christians that God wants them to trust and obey. Be God's heroic messenger.

Dear God, sometimes it's too easy to be quiet about You. It can seem like I'm embarrassed to know You, like You're not really important to me. Help me be courageous enough to share Your message with people who have never heard and those who have forgotten. Amen.

• •

BECOMING A HERO

○ Why do you think it was hard for Elijah to be a prophet hero?

○ Why do you think King Ahab considered Elijah a troublemaker?

○ What makes sharing God's message difficult for you?

○ How can sharing God's message bring you closer to God?

○ What is the opposite of being a prophet?

Integrity Means. . .

Elisha's Heroic Story

2 KINGS 5

22

Whoever walks in
integrity walks securely.

PROVERBS 10:9 NIV

71

Integrity means keeping your word and honoring a promise no matter how hard it might be. Integrity means doing the right thing even when there is no reward, pat on the back, or trophy. Integrity cares about being dependable and trustworthy, honorable and kind, and saying what is meant and keeping your promise.

If you're looking for a biblical hero of integrity, you should read the story of Elisha.

Elisha spoke for God. Like Elijah, Nathan, and Samuel, Elisha was a prophet. God told him what to say, and Elisha spoke those exact words.

One day a soldier named Naaman came to Elisha and expected the prophet to heal him of a skin disease. The soldier had no right to expect Elisha to heal him. The soldier did not know Elisha's God. The soldier treated the visit like you might treat a visit to the doctor.

Elisha could have sent Naaman home. Elisha could have reminded the soldier that he didn't honor God. Elisha could have treated the soldier without kindness. He could have. He didn't.

Elisha had his servant tell the soldier what to do. If the soldier followed Elisha's directions, he would be healed. If he was healed, he could thank God and give Him honor.

Naaman was not happy that Elisha sent his servant to talk to him. Naaman didn't want to follow the prophet's directions. Naaman thought he was more important than the God who could heal. When Naaman finally followed Elisha's directions, he was healed. Completely cured. His skin disease was gone.

Naaman wanted to thank Elisha. Elisha wanted Naaman to thank God. This was how Elisha showed integrity. When the soldier came back and offered to make Elisha a rich man, Elisha reminded Naaman that God healed him. Elisha had simply spoken God's prescription for healing. Elisha couldn't become rich by taking credit for something God had done. Elisha turned down Naaman's gifts.

Naaman must have thought it very strange that the prophet refused payment. When Elisha gave God credit, maybe it helped Naaman understand who really helped him.

Heroes of integrity give credit to those who do the work. They are honest when things don't work out the way they had hoped. They don't give up on promises. They honor God.

Elisha proved that he was secure because God made him secure. When you only trust in what you receive for the good things you do, you will often find yourself insecure.

Dear God, help me never take credit for the things You do.
Help me honor You by keeping my promises. May I be a hero
of integrity and someone who loves You enough to do my very
best. Help me find my security by keeping my integrity focused
on all You are, all You've said, and with all I am. Amen.

. . . .

BECOMING A HERO

O **Why do you think Naaman found it unusual for Elisha to refuse honor and gifts?**

O **Why do you think Elisha turned down Naaman's gifts?**

O **Why is it easy to want people to notice you when you do a good deed?**

O **What do you think is a good response when someone notices the heroic quality of integrity in you?**

O **What is the opposite of integrity?**

23

A King's Cooperation
Josiah's Heroic Story
2 KINGS 23; 2 CHRONICLES 34

Can two people walk together without agreeing on the direction?

AMOS 3:3 NLT

74

Josiah was only eight years old when he became king. He didn't know the people had not been cooperating with God. He didn't know God had rules to be followed. He didn't know the people had made God upset.

The people worshipped other gods, but Josiah didn't know that was wrong. The people behaved in ways that made God mad, but Josiah didn't know he should tell them to stop. The people did whatever they wanted, but Josiah didn't say anything because it was the only way he had ever seen the people behave.

That was before Josiah was told that a long-lost book had been found. That book was filled with God's words. When Josiah heard what was written in that book, he was sad and ashamed. The people had not been living the way God told them to live. Very few people knew that God had rules to be followed. Suddenly Josiah knew what needed to be done.

Josiah made a brave decision. Josiah wanted the people to know and follow God's rules. Josiah told the people to stop following any other god or worshipping any idols. Josiah cooperated with God and asked the people to do the same.

This young king was a hero of cooperation with God. Once Josiah knew what God wanted, he didn't question God; he didn't check for ways to avoid it; and he didn't tell God, "No!" Josiah did what God asked, and the people followed the king who cooperated with God.

God is always looking for men, women, boys, and girls who will cooperate with His plans. He wants to find people who will not stand in His way but will help Him do the good things He wants to do for people. He wants you to show love to others, follow His rules, and go where He sends you.

A hero who cooperates with God will need to read the Bible to know what God wants. Once you know what God wants, you will need to obey what He says. Once you do what He says, you become a hero of cooperation. You can also expect that God will continue to have new and exciting jobs you can do for Him.

When you decide you don't want to follow God, you cannot cooperate with Him. If you don't feel close to God, it could be that you have not been cooperating with Him. God has some pretty wonderful adventures for everyone willing to cooperate. Josiah cooperated, and it changed his entire nation. You can cooperate, too. Grab God's hand and walk with Him.

Dear God, I am sorry if I haven't been cooperating with You. I don't know everything You want me to do. Could You help me understand how to cooperate with Your plans when I read the Bible? Help me follow You. Help others see that following You is the best idea. I want to be someone who will cooperate with Your plans. Amen.

* *

BECOMING A HERO

O **Why do you think Josiah was sad when he learned he had not been cooperating with God?**

O **What did Josiah do that made him a hero?**

O **Why do you think you don't always cooperate with God?**

O **What makes it hard to be a hero of cooperation?**

O **What is the opposite of cooperation?**

Bold and Believing

Hezekiah's Heroic Story

2 CHRONICLES 29–32

Since God assured us, "I'll never let you down, never walk off and leave you," we can boldly quote, God is there, ready to help; I'm fearless no matter what. Who or what can get to me?

HEBREWS 13:5–6 MSG

When people say, "No one believes in God anymore," they usually mean they think God is an ancient idea that seems like a fairy tale. They might feel smart by saying God is made up. This is the same God who made the world, created you, and offers daily help. If you think this is the first time people thought God wasn't real, you should read about a bold hero named Hezekiah.

Hezekiah grew up hearing that the idea of God no longer made sense. Hezekiah's dad, Ahaz, closed the temple and sent the priests home. He wanted people to stop thinking about God. He wanted them to worship anything but God. He didn't want the people to love God. For years it seemed like Ahaz succeeded.

His son, Hezekiah, wanted to know about God. Maybe he disagreed with his dad. When Hezekiah became king, one of the first things he did was find a way to open the doors to the forgotten temple. Workers were hired to clean. Workers were hired to repair. Workers were hired to destroy the idols people thought had replaced God. The priests returned to their work.

King Hezekiah didn't just repair the temple. He didn't just destroy the idols. He sent an invitation to those who had forgotten God to come back. Hezekiah wanted the people to worship God. He was bold in asking them to come together to learn about God.

Because the king was bold, the people were reintroduced to God. Because Hezekiah cared more about what God thought than what people thought, he followed God even when it didn't make sense to others. Because Hezekiah was bold, he encourages people like you to love God—no matter what.

You can be a hero who is not ashamed to let others know you follow God. Hebrews 11:1 (NIV) says, "Faith is confidence in what we hope for and assurance about what we do not see." To be confident and assured means that you can really believe in God whether anyone agrees with you or not.

When you care more about pleasing God than what other people think, you are becoming a hero of boldness like King Hezekiah.

God wants to be close to the people He loves. When you are bold, you can introduce God to people He wants to rescue.

Dear God, is it possible You want bold heroes who love to let people know You love them? Could it be there is no reason to fear those who think You are an ancient idea? Help me love You enough to become bold enough to share You enough. Give me the strength to believe in You when others wrongly think it's not worth my time. Amen.

● ●

BECOMING A HERO

○ **Why would it have been hard for Hezekiah to open the temple after his father closed the doors for so many years?**

○ **How did reopening the temple show the heroic quality of boldness?**

○ **What can you do to be bold for God?**

○ **Why is honoring God more important than impressing people?**

○ **What is the opposite of boldness?**

25

God's Plan, Nehemiah's Purpose

Nehemiah's Heroic Story

THE BOOK OF NEHEMIAH

Fear God.
Do what he tells you.
ECCLESIASTES 12:13 MSG

Nehemiah was a servant in Babylon. He worked for the king. He made sure the king was refreshed. God had a new job for Nehemiah, and it meant returning to the land where his family lived.

When Babylon came to the land of Israel, there were very few people left in Jerusalem. The temple had been destroyed. No one tried to fix it. Nehemiah was sad. The temple was where people worshipped God. People needed to worship God again.

The people of Israel had been sent by God to Babylon to learn to obey Him once more. God had promised they could come back to Israel, but with the temple destroyed Nehemiah was not sure what would be left when the people came home.

Nehemiah prayed that God would help him talk to the king of Babylon. God helped. Nehemiah asked the king to let him go back to Jerusalem. The king helped. When Nehemiah saw the work that needed to be done, he asked people living in Jerusalem to help. The people helped.

Asking Nehemiah to rebuild the walls would be like asking a baker to run a bank, a seamstress to build a park, or a king to be a plumber. It wasn't the job he had always had, but God gave him a new purpose. By accepting his new job, Nehemiah became a hero of purpose.

Nehemiah learned. Nehemiah had help. Nehemiah built a wall and repaired the temple. God could use someone who refreshed a king to refresh Jerusalem. The people didn't realize it, but the hero of purpose was making sure things were prepared for the day when the people would leave Babylon and finally come home to Israel.

Sometimes your family will ask you to try something you've never tried before. That can be scary. You might think you will fail. You don't want to be embarrassed. Trying something you've never done before could help you learn God's purpose for your life. You will learn what you like and what you don't like. You can learn the things you're really good at and those things that take some work. You will learn that sometimes the thing God made you to do will be hard work, but it will leave you satisfied.

God has a plan for your life. When you follow His plan, you have a purpose. When you have a purpose, God provides everything you need to do the work. Don't be surprised when God sends help.

Honor God. Do what He tells you.

Dear God, when I wonder why I'm here and what I'm supposed to do, help me remember that You made me and had a plan for me before I was even born. You help those who need help— and I need help. Give me the strength to try new things. Help me discover the purpose behind my life. May I do what You ask so I can be the person You made me to be. Amen.

• •

BECOMING A HERO

○ **Why was Nehemiah so concerned about the wall and temple in Jerusalem?**

○ **What hard thing did Nehemiah have to do before he could go to Jerusalem?**

○ **Why is it hard for you to try new things?**

○ **What new thing have you tried that you really like?**

○ **What is the opposite of purpose?**

26

Scared but Brave
Esther's Heroic Story
ESTHER 1–5

The wicked flee though no one pursues, but the righteous are as bold as a lion.

PROVERBS 28:1 NIV

Esther was part of the Bible's first beauty contest. She won. Her prize? She became queen over all the land. She didn't come from a well-known family. She didn't act as if she were more beautiful than any other young woman. Esther had no plans to become queen, but the king liked her and *he* was judging the contest.

Haman worked for the king. He wasn't like Esther. He wanted to be noticed. He wanted the king to like him. He wanted to be known as the man the king always called when he needed advice.

Haman didn't want the king to notice anyone else. He hated when people didn't treat him as if *he* had won a contest. When Esther's close relative Mordecai refused to treat him as if he *were* the king, Haman had an evil thought. He wanted Mordecai to die. Haman lied to the king. He said there was an enemy in the kingdom. He said there was an entire family of people who hated the king. Haman even promised to help pay to fight this enemy. The king thought Haman was telling the truth, so he signed a law allowing the evil Haman to wage war with an enemy that was never really an enemy. Haman started a war because he was mad at Mordecai. Haman didn't know Mordecai had once saved the king's life. Haman didn't know Queen Esther was part of Mordecai's family.

Esther is a hero of bravery because when she discovered what Haman had done, she knew she had to tell the king that his new law meant Haman could kill *her*. He could kill her family. But there was a big problem. In order to see the king, Esther would need to be called to come see him. He hadn't called. If she went to see the king on her own, she could be put to death if he didn't want to see her. Esther bravely chose to see the king on her own. She asked her family to pray for her. God was with Esther, and the king was eager to hear what she had to say.

Because she was brave, Esther's family was allowed to protect themselves and the king made Mordecai a leader in his kingdom. Haman was punished for his evil plan.

Being brave means you stand up for what's right. It means you face the things that make you scared. Being brave means being so sure you're on God's side that you can't imagine turning your back on His truth.

Dear God, help me to be brave. It's easier to stay quiet even when I know Your way is better. It's easier to run away when things get tough. It's easier to hope for the best while I stand back and refuse to help. I want to be brave, but I can't do this alone. Amen.

BECOMING A HERO

O   **What are two differences between Queen Esther and Haman?**

O   **Why did Queen Esther need to be so brave just to visit the king?**

O   **What are some of the things that make being brave hard?**

O   **Who are you most like: Esther, Mordecai, or Haman? Why?**

O   **What is the opposite of being brave?**

27

Prepared and on Assignment

Mordecai's Heroic Story

THE BOOK OF ESTHER

Take a lesson from the ants.
. . . Learn from their ways
and become wise! . . .
They labor hard all summer.

PROVERBS 6:6–8 NLT

Have you ever done something kind for someone but not been thanked for your help? It happens to God every day. It also happened to a man named Mordecai—and he saved a king.

If you read the story of Queen Esther, then you know that Mordecai was her relative. He cared about the king and didn't want him to get hurt. So, when Mordecai heard two men named Bigthana and Teresh talking about a plan to kill the king, he knew he had to warn the king.

Mordecai was kind, and King Xerxes was saved. King Xerxes did not immediately say thank you, though. It seemed the king forgot the kindness. Mordecai did not get mad. Mordecai did not tell people the king was unkind. Mordecai simply went back to work.

Mordecai was preparing to be useful to God. If he had become bitter, he would not have been able to hear God speak. If he had become angry, he would have acted like Haman. If he had wanted to get back at King Xerxes, he would have acted like Bigthana and Teresh. He had done the right thing, and now he waited for God's next assignment.

One night the king had trouble sleeping. He asked that someone read from his big record book. As he listened, the king was reminded of the kindness of Mordecai. That's when Haman showed up to tell the king how horrible Mordecai was. Before Haman could speak, the king asked Haman to help him decide what should be done to show honor to someone who had been helpful to him. Haman didn't know the king was talking about Mordecai. Haman thought the king was talking about him. Haman gave many helpful suggestions, thinking it was the best day ever. He thought he would be the one honored. Imagine his surprise when the king accepted every one of his ideas and told him to be the very person to treat Mordecai in this honorable way. Haman became even bitterer, angrier, and more upset.

Mordecai was a hero of preparation. He prepared for God's good gifts. He didn't wait to be thanked by the king. Haman was preparing to hurt Mordecai, and God gave him the reward of the wicked.

Mordecai did the right thing. Haman chose the wrong thing. Mordecai was honored. Haman was humiliated.

Doing the right things means you prepare. You decide ahead of time how you will respond to everything that seems unfair. You decide ahead of time how you will treat others. You decide ahead of time whom you will trust when life is hard. Be prepared.

Dear God, sometimes I ask for Your help when I get into trouble. When Mordecai prepared, he made some choices a long time before most people would. Help me be more like that. Help me decide how I will act before bad things happen. Help me trust You when others are unkind. Amen.

• •

BECOMING A HERO

○ **What did you like most about Mordecai?**

○ **Why is Mordecai a hero of preparation?**

○ **Why is it hard to be kind when people don't thank you for being helpful?**

○ **How can you prepare for your next bad day?**

○ **What is the opposite of being prepared?**

Patience Required

Job's Heroic Story
THE BOOK OF JOB

28

Be joyful in hope, patient in affliction, faithful in prayer.

ROMANS 12:12 NIV

The easiest way to tell if you've learned a lesson is to see if you're patient when you stumble into the same problem again. Patience is a gift to those who've been through a struggle and discovered they can survive.

Sometimes you have to deal with problems that aren't your fault. Those kinds of problems really need patience. You can learn more about patience in the story of Job (his name rhymes with *robe*).

God had a very good opinion of Job. He was smart with his money. He prayed for his children. He honored God. But mankind's worst enemy, Satan, wanted to test Job. He wanted Job to fail. He went to God and said that the only reason Job wasn't the worst man alive was that God had given him so much.

It's true that Job did have lots of land, animals, and children. It's true that Job was healthy and happy. It's true that people looked up to Job and asked him for advice. Satan thought that if good things were taken from Job, then he would be angry with God.

God allowed Satan to take things from Job. Job was very sad. He wondered what went wrong. He prayed to God for answers. But Job did not stop believing in God. He still honored God in what he said, how he acted, and with all he had left.

It can be hard to be a hero of patience when bad days add up to bad weeks. You might be willing to face a bad day every once in a while, but when it seems that good days never come, it's hard to be patient.

Job was like you. He didn't like bad days. He didn't know that Satan was making the days bad. Job didn't know that God was watching him very carefully to see if he still trusted Him. The hero of patience was getting weaker every day.

Job's friends were sure he had sinned. They were sure he was doing things to make God mad. They weren't being very good friends.

When God helped Job understand, his strength returned. He trusted God even when things didn't make sense. God gave Job more than he lost. God showed love to Job. God grew Job's family, and Job loved each new member.

On days when you struggle most, remember God loves you and He will never stop loving you. Be patient. Your worst day can bring you closer to God. Your worst moments will help you remember you've had better moments. Bad times help you praise God for the good times. Be patient. This won't last forever.

Dear God, I admit it. Sometimes I'm impatient. I don't like to wait. I don't like to wonder if tomorrow will be a good day. Help me be patient. Help me remember that even when things look bad, You can make them good. Help me trust that even when I don't like what I'm going through, You go through it with me. Amen.

. . . .

BECOMING A HERO

O **Did it seem unfair that Job had so many bad days? Why?**

O **What do you think Job learned by being a hero of patience?**

O **Why is it so hard for you to be patient?**

O **What makes patience such a heroic quality?**

O **What is the opposite of patience?**

29

There Is Hope

Isaiah's Heroic Story

2 KINGS 20; THE BOOK OF ISAIAH

[God said], "I know what I'm doing. I have it all planned out—plans to take care of you, not abandon you, plans to give you the future you hope for."

JEREMIAH 29:11 MSG

There are sixty-six chapters in the book of Isaiah, and the most important thing Isaiah had to say was, "There is hope."

Most of the book of Isaiah has words about justice and capture, punishment and homelessness. Isaiah was a prophet. He spoke for God. Isaiah didn't just write about the end of a good life in Israel; he wrote about God's plan to mend Israel. That would take awhile. God would give the people a seventy-year *time-out* in Babylon.

The people needed time to stop believing the lies they kept telling themselves. They would need time to learn to worship God once more. They would need to stop believing they could do whatever they wanted without God knowing.

God was not okay with the choices the people were making. That's why a few verses in Isaiah 53 prove Isaiah was a hero of hope. God told Isaiah there would be a day when His Son would make it possible for men, women, boys, and girls to be forgiven for the wrong choice of sin.

Isaiah wrote, "It was our pains [Jesus] carried. . .all the things wrong with us. We thought he brought it on himself, that God was punishing him for his own failures. But it was our sins that did that to him. . .our sins! He took the punishment, and that made us whole. Through his bruises we get healed. We're all like sheep who've wandered off and gotten lost. We've all done our own thing, gone our own way. And GOD has piled all our sins, everything we've done wrong, on him, on him" (Isaiah 53:4–6 MSG).

When Isaiah wrote God's words about the people being sent to Babylon, his country had a good leader. King Hezekiah was a hero of boldness, but God still had plans to send the people away from Israel. People may have thought Isaiah only liked to share bad news. They might have thought Isaiah couldn't see that things were pretty good. The people were slowly walking away from God. They lost their way. They wouldn't follow directions. What Isaiah had to say was true, but no one wanted to believe it.

If people had really understood what Isaiah was saying, they should have praised God for His plan to send Jesus to forgive sin. They would have understood that God was making everything ready for the world's best rescue plan. They could have understood that Isaiah had the best message of hope anyone had ever heard.

Dear God, when bad things happen, I can still hope in You. When I don't think I can take another step, You give me strength. You want me to understand that there is no one I could follow who is a better leader, no one who loves me more, and no one who could forgive my sin. Help me see that with You, I always have hope. Amen.

• •

BECOMING A HERO

○ **What was Isaiah's best hope?**

○ **Why do you think some people didn't believe what Isaiah said?**

○ **How can you become a hero of hope?**

○ **How is hope different than a wish?**

○ **What is the opposite of hope?**

30

A Dedicated Message
Jeremiah's Heroic Story
THE BOOK OF JEREMIAH

Don't just listen to God's word. You must do what it says. Otherwise, you are only fooling yourselves.

JAMES 1:22 NLT

God had a message. He asked Jeremiah to share it. Jeremiah didn't think he was old enough, brave enough, or strong enough to do what God asked. He was scared, and he made sure God knew it.

But that didn't stop God. He promised to be with Jeremiah and give him the words he should speak. Jeremiah wasn't the only messenger or prophet to share God's message, but God's message made Jeremiah sad.

The message didn't seem kind. It didn't seem encouraging. The message spoke of an enemy coming into his country and taking the people captive. This was God's message. This was part of what Jeremiah was supposed to say when he spoke to people.

Some people thought Jeremiah was a troublemaker. Some laughed at him. Some just wanted him to be quiet. But hadn't God said, "Do not be afraid. I will go with you"?

The king in charge was a good king. People found it hard to believe Jeremiah's message. King Josiah followed God and reopened the temple. People wondered why God would judge a nation that was doing the right things.

It was true; King Josiah was following God with all that was in his heart, with every bit of his strength, and with every thought in his mind. But the people did not follow God in the same way. They did the right things, but they did not honor God like their king. They made it look like they loved God, but inside they pushed Him away.

As soon as Josiah died, the people no longer tried to act as if they loved God. They went back to living as if the only thing that mattered was what they wanted to believe.

The people would be sent to Babylon, and the king of that country treated Jeremiah with more kindness than the people of Judah.

Jeremiah is a hero of dedication because God had given him a message no one wanted to hear, yet Jeremiah shared it. He spoke God's words on good days, bad days, and on the days when Babylon invaded. His message was not popular. People were tired of hearing it. They no longer believed what God had to say was worth listening to. And still, Jeremiah spoke God's words.

You can be a hero of dedication, too. To be dedicated means you believe following God is more important than anything. It means you make obedience to God's rules a goal. It means you will not believe or follow things that do not honor God.

Dear God, forgive me for ever considering that You are just an option—as if I could follow You if I felt like it or set You aside like an old toy. You're worth following every moment of every day. Help me treat Your plans for my life the same way Jeremiah did. Help me pay attention to what You say so I can do what You ask. Amen.

• •

BECOMING A HERO

○ How are you like Jeremiah?

○ Why do you think what God asked Jeremiah to do was so hard for him?

○ When have you struggled with doing the right thing? What did you do?

○ Would you consider yourself a hero of dedication? Why?

○ What is the opposite of dedication?

31

Sermons God Wrote

Ezekiel's Heroic Story

The Book of Ezekiel

Preach the word; be prepared in season and out of season; correct, rebuke and encourage— with great patience and careful instruction.

2 Timothy 4:2 NIV

God sent His message of justice to the land of Israel and Judah. Isaiah and Jeremiah had been sharing this message with all who would listen, and to many who refused to listen. Once the army of Babylon took people away from their land, a new messenger began to speak. Ezekiel preached sermons God had written.

This prophet was sent to Babylon eight years after the first group of people were taken. Ezekiel didn't change the message God gave him just because he was in a new country. Like every real prophet, Ezekiel only said what God told him to say—and Ezekiel had lots of people to talk to. Ezekiel had lots of things to say.

Ezekiel was sad because some of the people taken to Babylon were acting like they had always lived in Babylon. They didn't act like they had been captured. They paid no attention to Ezekiel's words. They wanted to be just like the people who had captured them.

God told Ezekiel these people would not listen to Him. They had become too much like Babylon and not enough like the children of God. Ezekiel was asked to keep preaching the good sermon God had written for His people.

God had also written a sermon for Ezekiel to preach to those who made fun of the people of Israel and Judah. God was not pleased when people thought it was funny that the people of Israel had been taken captive. God wanted these people to know He would always be with His people—even when they made wrong choices—when they were being punished.

The third sermon God wrote for Ezekiel was a message of promise. Ezekiel told the people that God would bring them home. They had been living with the consequences of sin, but God would restore. God would make hard hearts soft once more. He would rescue His people, and they would learn to obey. This was a good sermon.

Ezekiel would not preach something that God had not written. It made him a hero. It may be different to think of a preaching hero, but "preaching hero" was something that described Ezekiel perfectly.

You can be a hero of preaching when you remember that God wants to belong in the words you say and the things you do. A preacher knows the truth, speaks the truth, and lives life in a way that matches God's truth.

Dear God, truth is important to You. If I tell something that is untrue, I do not speak for You. You wrote sermons on truth, and Ezekiel preached them to the people. Help me make the words of my mouth please You, and allow me to serve You well. Amen.

- -

BECOMING A HERO

O **Why can you think of Ezekiel as a preaching hero?**

O **Why is it important that Ezekiel spoke the truth when he preached?**

O **What can you do today that will help you be a preaching hero?**

O **Can you honor God by telling something you know is not true? Why?**

O **What is the opposite of preaching?**

The Only One to Trust

Daniel's Heroic Story

Daniel 6

32

The Lord is your security.

PROVERBS 3:26 NLT

To be confident means you feel certain that someone or something can be trusted. You might be confident that a car can get you to where you want to go—until the car breaks down. That's when you're not so certain. You could be confident that someone else will always be your friend—until they move and you miss them. You could be confident in your own abilities, but one poor decision can make you think you're not as trustworthy as you thought.

Is there anyone who can make you confident? Yes. God.

Daniel was a hero of confidence. He trusted God. King Darius liked Daniel and made him an important leader. The only person who was more important than Daniel was King Darius himself. It seemed like Daniel should have had confidence in the king. Daniel liked the king. Daniel did not think the king would do anything to harm him. But Daniel's confidence was only in God.

One day, men who were jealous of Daniel went to King Darius. They thought there should be a new rule that no one should pray to anyone but the king for an entire month. Maybe the king thought it was good to have people pray to him. Maybe he forgot that Daniel only prayed to God. Maybe the king was too busy with other things and just agreed so the men would leave.

The new law had a punishment for anyone who prayed to anyone but the king. If a person was discovered disobeying the law, they would be thrown into a pit of wild lions. These lions killed men. These lions were hungry.

The jealous men watched Daniel to see what he would do. They saw him kneel and pray to God. Daniel wasn't confident in trusting these men. They went straight to the king and told him what Daniel had done. They reminded the king that the law could not be overlooked. The king was sad, but he called Daniel and had him thrown into the pit with the lions.

The jealous men thought they had won. The king knew he had made a bad decision in making the new law. Daniel prayed. He was confident in God.

God sent angels to keep the lions' mouths closed. God made the wild lions tame for the night. The lions did not harm Daniel at all.

Daniel put his confidence in God. King Darius saw how strong God really is.

Being confident in what God can do is always the right choice. He never lets His family down. He wants what's best for you. Trust Him. Follow Him. He can be trusted with your hardest choices.

Dear God, when I have no confidence in myself, when I struggle to trust others, help me remember that I can be confident in You. You know the plans for my life, and You lead me in the right directions. You can be trusted—so I trust You. Amen.

• •

BECOMING A HERO

O   **Why do you think Daniel is a hero of confidence?**

O   **Do you think you would have prayed to God knowing it was against the law? Why?**

O   **Why is it hard to be confident in friends?**

O   **Why is it hard to be confident in yourself?**

O   **What is the opposite of confidence?**

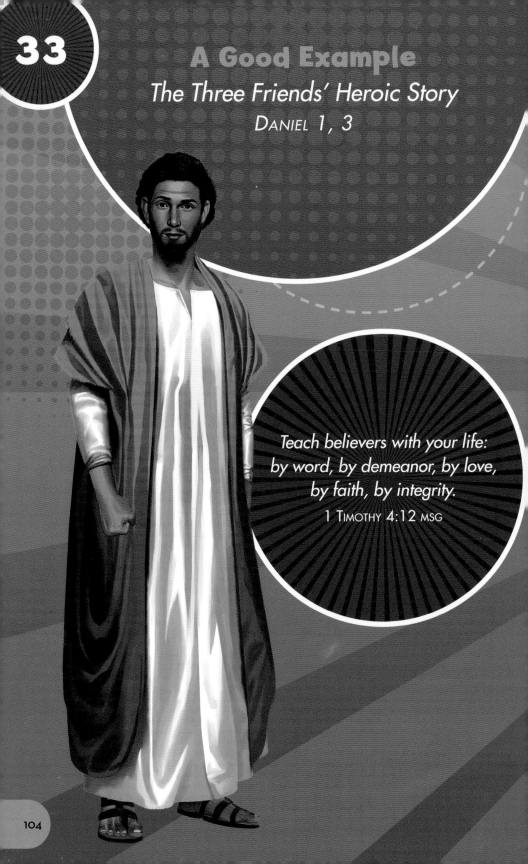

33

A Good Example
The Three Friends' Heroic Story
DANIEL 1, 3

*Teach believers with your life:
by word, by demeanor, by love,
by faith, by integrity.*
1 TIMOTHY 4:12 MSG

Three boys had been born in Israel. They became good friends. They loved God and followed Him. When they were still young, their country was invaded by the armies of Babylon. The three boys were taken away from their homes. Shadrach, Meshach, and Abednego weren't the only boys taken, but they became heroes of example.

Their story starts with food. The king said that all the young men would eat what he ate and drink what he drank. The three friends knew that the king's food was not what God had told them to eat. While other boys ate the king's food, Shadrach, Meshach, and Abednego asked if they could eat food they knew God wanted them to eat.

In ten days, the three looked healthier than those who had eaten the king's food. They followed God in small things. Then God had bigger plans for Shadrach, Meshach, and Abednego.

The king liked the three and made them leaders. As they grew to be men, the king built a statue and demanded that everyone bow to it when they heard special music.

Being heroes of example, Shadrach, Meshach, and Abednego knew that God had said they should not worship anyone but God. They knew they could not do what the king asked.

The king liked these three friends, so he gave them a second chance. They still refused. The king did not like it when people refused his commands.

The king was angry. He had a furnace burning nearby and ordered his soldiers to make the furnace seven times hotter than usual. Fire spilled from the furnace, and red, orange, and yellow flames stretched above the furnace doors. The king's soldiers threw Shadrach, Meshach, and Abednego into the fire. These three friends were supposed to die, but God had other plans. These three honored God, and God saved them from the fire.

The king watched. The soldiers watched. The people watched. What they saw were *four* men walking in the red, orange, and yellow flames. The king was sure only Shadrach, Meshach, and Abednego were thrown into the fire, but there was one more, and He was different than the other three. The king was amazed none of the three friends were hurt. The king no longer wanted to hurt the men. He wanted to know more about the fourth man. He wanted to know more about the God they served. The example of Shadrach, Meshach, and Abednego was recognized by the king. God was pleased.

You can be an example to others. God can protect you, help you, and use you to show others that following God is the most important command you can follow.

Dear God, You are my best example on how to live, why I should love, and how to forgive. Help me discover ways I can be an example to others. May my life look a lot like Your example. May people who see me follow You. Amen.

• •

BECOMING A HERO

O **Name two ways Shadrach, Meshach, and Abednego were heroes of example.**

O **Why do you think God can use boys and girls who follow His example?**

O **How can you be an example to someone today?**

O **Why is it hard to be an example?**

O **What is the opposite of example?**

34

Two Messages and One Amazing Rescue

Gabriel's Heroic Story

LUKE 1

"I bring you good news that will bring great joy to all people."

LUKE 2:10 NLT

Jesus is God's only Son. Jesus had always been with God. When Adam and Eve disobeyed God, there was a plan to forgive every sinful act that men, women, and children would ever choose. This plan would require a sacrifice. This sacrifice would need to be perfect. Jesus was perfect.

God knew that it would mean Jesus would die for sin on a cross. God knew that Jesus would rise from the dead. God knew this was the only way to repair a broken relationship with men, women, and children who chose sin instead of obedience.

Very few people understood who Jesus was, but God had a plan to help them understand. He would send one of His messenger angels. Gabriel was God's choice.

God gave Gabriel two messages. The first message was delivered to a priest named Zechariah. This priest was not a young man. Most of his friends were grandparents, but Gabriel's message was very unexpected. Zechariah was going to become a dad. His wife, Elizabeth, was going to have a baby. His name would be John. This boy grew up and made sure people knew that Jesus was coming.

It wasn't long before Gabriel delivered his second message. This time he spoke to a young woman named Mary. God had a great plan for Mary.

Gabriel told her that she would have a baby. Gabriel told her this baby was God's Son. Gabriel told Mary that this boy had a very special purpose. This boy would be King.

John grew and told everyone he met that Jesus was coming soon. John was ready to step back so Jesus could step forward and change the world. Jesus grew and rescued people from their choice to sin.

The message about John and Jesus was delivered by a messenger hero named Gabriel. The message was from God. It was a message Gabriel was chosen to deliver. The message was a plan that was only understood after Jesus died and rose from the dead. God loves people and wants to be close to us.

You've read about prophets like Jeremiah, Elijah, and Ezekiel. They all shared God's messages. So did Gabriel. To share God's messages, you have to obey God. You must share His message, not your own. You must know the message, not guess. You must follow the One who gave the message, not walk away thinking God's message isn't worth sharing.

Dear God, You did not want Your message to be a secret. You sent Gabriel to give Your message to the ones who needed to hear it. Help me remember that You don't ask for a crowd in order to share Your message. Sometimes Your greatest messages are shared with one person who really needs to hear it. Help me share what You want to share with anyone You want me to share it with. Amen.

• •

BECOMING A HERO

○ **Why would it be hard to believe an angel brought you a message from God?**

○ **Should Gabriel have been honored to share God's message? Why?**

○ **Truth is one of God's messages. Have you ever felt God is asking you to share truth? What did you do?**

○ **Why should you think it's possible God wants you to be a messenger today?**

○ **What is the opposite of sharing God's message?**

35

Willing to Serve
Mary's Heroic Story
LUKE 1–2

"Fear the LORD and faithfully serve him. Think of all the wonderful things he has done for you."
1 SAMUEL 12:24 NLT

The emperor ordered everyone to go back to their family city. Once everyone arrived, the officials would count the people to see how many belonged to each family. Then everyone would need to pay a tax. No one could have an excuse to stay home.

Mary's husband, Joseph, was part of King David's family. That meant he and Mary had to travel many miles to a small city called Bethlehem. Mary was going to be a mom. It was not a good time for a woman who was going to have a baby to travel. There were more people in town than ever. When Mary and Joseph arrived, there was no room for them in any home, guesthouse, or inn. Jesus would be born very soon. The couple found a place to rest in a stable. It wasn't the perfect place for a baby to be born, but the story of His unusual birth is still told today.

God had sent the angel Gabriel to tell Mary she would give birth to God's Son. Once Jesus was born, Mary wrapped the baby boy in strips of cloth to keep Him warm. Jesus slept His first night in Bethlehem in a manger. A manger was where cows usually ate their meals. That night it was a crib.

Mary probably wanted something better for baby Jesus. Most people thought Mary had a difficult life. But Mary remembered God's plan. She was a hero of willingness, and God helped her.

When the angel Gabriel shared God's big idea with Mary, the young woman was willing to do what God asked her to do. Mary didn't know how to be a mom. She didn't know what it would be like to raise God's Son. She didn't know all of God's plan. Mary only knew what the angel had said, and it was enough. Mary was willing.

God has something He wants you to do. The job will always seem bigger, harder, and bolder than you think you can handle. Don't be surprised if God offers His help when you offer your willingness. He will always do what you can't. He will always help when nothing seems to make sense.

God helps those who are willing to do what He asks. He helps those who are willing to receive His help.

Dear God, some things you asked people to do in the Bible seemed impossible. Elijah healed a sick man. Noah built the ark. Mary brought Jesus into the world. What do You want me to do? Help me understand Your plans for me—and then help me to be willing to follow Your plan, ask for Your help, and do what You ask. Amen.

- -

BECOMING A HERO

O **What ways can you think of that might have made it hard for Mary to be a hero of willingness?**

O **Mary was willing to obey, but did that make things easier? Why or why not?**

O **What gifts can God give to those who are willing to follow His plan?**

O **You've read about many people who were willing to do what God asked. How does their willingness encourage you to do the same?**

O **What is the opposite of being willing?**

Joseph's Heroic Story
MATTHEW 1; LUKE 2

We live by believing
and not by seeing.
2 CORINTHIANS 5:7 NLT

Joseph would become the husband of Mary. Mary would become the mother of Jesus. Jesus was *God's* one and only Son.

If you're confused, imagine how Joseph felt. Like Mary, Joseph had been visited by an angel. Joseph was asked to be committed to Mary, and to the baby boy who was to be born. Joseph did not know of other men who would help raise a child who was not their own, but Joseph took a brave step toward becoming a committed hero. Mary became his wife, and Joseph loved Jesus as if He were his own child.

A little more than a week had passed since Jesus was born in a stable. Eight days since the shepherds came and witnessed God's miracle. Eight days since the innkeeper said, "No room." The baby was taken to the temple to be dedicated to God. Joseph was poor and could only offer two doves to dedicate Jesus, but Jesus was *God's* Son. It was enough.

A man and a woman who were old enough to be Joseph's grandparents saw Jesus and recognized Him as the one God had promised would save the people. These two treated Jesus as a king. They honored a boy who still had to learn to speak.

Wise men came to honor the boy. King Herod tried to kill Him. Joseph remembered his commitment to care for Jesus, and he took Mary and Jesus to Egypt where they were safe from the king's bad law.

Years later, when Jesus was twelve years old, Joseph took Him to Jerusalem with his mother, Mary. There they would remember how God saved His people from an Egyptian pharaoh many, many years before. It was a special time. People celebrated. They ate together. They sang songs. They remembered. They went home.

Joseph didn't know Jesus had stayed in Jerusalem and was teaching the religious leaders. Joseph may have thought Jesus was playing with friends. He may have thought Jesus was exploring on the way home. He did not think Jesus had stayed behind to help the teachers of the Law learn things about God that they didn't know. When Joseph discovered Jesus was missing, he was committed to finding the boy. When Joseph found Jesus, he remembered that Jesus was God's Son. His real Father had plans for the boy that Joseph did not know.

There will be times when God's plans mean you will have something new to do for Him. You can be a hero of commitment when you learn His plan, follow His path, and stick with His instructions.

Dear God, being committed means I follow You without changing my mind. Help me be committed. Following You means You have a direction. Help me pay attention. Your direction means You have a plan for my life. Help me thank You for thinking of me. Because You love me, help me be committed to following Your plan. Amen.

• •

BECOMING A HERO

O **Why might it have been difficult for Joseph to be committed to God's plan?**

O **What are two ways Joseph proved he was committed to following God?**

O **Why is it hard to do something you've never done before?**

O **How can you show your commitment to God?**

O **What is the opposite of commitment?**

37

He Stepped Back

John the Baptist's Heroic Story

MATTHEW 3; JOHN 3:27–36

"Do you want to stand out? Then step down. Be a servant. If you puff yourself up, you'll get the wind knocked out of you. But if you're content to simply be yourself, your life will count for plenty."

MATTHEW 23:11–12 MSG

Crowds gathered to hear what John the Baptist would say. His words always made people think. Some people liked his words. Some people were angry. But John said words God had given him to say.

There were lots of men named John, so John had a little extra added to his name. He wasn't John the tanner or John the seller of pottery. He was John the one who baptizes—or John the Baptist for short.

John lived in the wilderness. His clothes were made from the hide of camels. He ate locusts and honey. People thought he looked a little wild. He probably did.

John was the son God promised to the priest Zechariah and his wife, Elizabeth. He was the one God had chosen to prepare people to meet His Son, Jesus.

The crowds proved people wanted to hear what John said. He was becoming very popular. He was remembered for his words. However, when Jesus came to be baptized by John, something changed.

John became a hero of humility. He knew Jesus was the most important person anyone would ever know. He didn't feel worthy to baptize Jesus. John only wanted to honor God's Son. Once John baptized Jesus, God said, "My Son pleases me. I love Him."

John knew he had finished the job God had created him to do. The people loved John, but John loved God more. John left the crowds. He encouraged people to follow Jesus. He stopped speaking in the wilderness.

John might have become more popular if he had continued preaching to the crowds, but Jesus had a new message, and the people needed to hear it. If this were a stage play, John would have stepped back so Jesus could walk into the spotlight.

John was humble enough to want what God wanted. He stepped down from his job because it was finished. He could be happy that Jesus had come to save the world from the sin that kept them from God.

You will always do the right thing by remembering God is most important. What He wants is more important than what you want. His plans are more important than yours. To be a hero of humility, you let God shine and you follow His plans.

Dear God, You know more than I ever will. You created the world and all the stars. You want to be close to people just like me. When I am humble, I remember You always do what I can't. You loved me before I loved You. You forgave when I needed forgiveness. I should want what You want because You have always known what I need. Amen.

- -

BECOMING A HERO

O **John the Baptist was popular. Why do you think it might have been hard for him to step away from fame?**

O **In what ways do you think John made sure everything was ready for Jesus to change the world?**

O **What does humility mean to you?**

O **Can you remember a time when you needed to be humble? How did it make you feel?**

O **What is the opposite of humility?**

Love Is the Reason

Jesus' Heroic Story

THE BOOK OF LUKE

38

We love because
he first loved us.

1 JOHN 4:19 NIV

Jesus was right beside God watching the very first sunrise earth had ever known. He had always been with God. Jesus knew every person whose story was told in the Bible. He knew everyone else, too. Jesus was just as important as God, but He stepped away from some of what it was like to be God's Son to become a human baby.

Jesus didn't become someone like you just because He was curious about what it was like to cry or play outdoor games with friends. Jesus came and became human because mankind walked away from God. They did whatever made them happy, and everyone broke God's rules. It all started with the first man and woman, Adam and Eve. It never stopped. Everyone has disobeyed God. Everyone.

The way back to God would need a repaired path. This would become the only way to find God. Jesus created the way. People still follow it today.

Jesus was human, but He never broke God's rules—not even once. He was the only perfect human who ever lived. Remember, Jesus knew that because He was just like God, the part of Him that was God would live forever. Jesus also knew that because He became a human, His human body would not live forever. When the time was right, Jesus allowed His body to be sacrificed on a cross. Because Jesus was perfect, His human death meant God could forgive the disobedience of men, women, boys, and girls.

If Jesus had not come, forgiveness would only be something we hoped for. Becoming a child of God would be impossible. No one would be worthy of living with God forever.

Jesus is the hero of love. He came to earth as a baby. He told the truth. He was misunderstood. He died on a cross. He rose again. He's alive, and He still helps people find the true path to God that He made a long time ago.

Love is the reason Jesus came. He loves you. He knew your name before you were born. He knows how many hairs are on your head. There is nothing about you that He doesn't know. And every time you break one of God's rules, Jesus invites you to walk with Him back in God's direction.

There is never a reason to hide from God. The best thing you can do is follow Jesus and admit to God that you've sinned. Accept His love, and follow the wonderful plan He has for you.

Why is this possible? Because Jesus has always loved you.

Dear God, thank You for sending Jesus. Thank You for the Bible that gives me directions on how to follow You. Thank You for loving me enough to make a way for me to find forgiveness for my disobedience, hope for my future, and help for everything I will face today. May I love You with the thankfulness of someone who has been given the best gift ever. Amen.

• •

BECOMING A HERO

O **Why do you think Jesus' love for you is so important?**

O **Why do you think Jesus felt it was important to help people find God?**

O **How do you know when someone really loves you?**

O **How can you show real love to others?**

O **What is the opposite of love?**

39

The Sincere Disciple
John's Heroic Story
Matthew 4

We prove ourselves by our purity, our understanding, our patience, our kindness, by the Holy Spirit within us, and by our sincere love.
2 Corinthians 6:6 NLT

John loved to fish. Fishing was his job, and he was good at it. He learned to fish from his father. He loved to fish with his brother. He loved the boat and the nets. Fishing was his life.

One day Jesus saw John, walked up to him, and said two words that invited John on his greatest adventure. Jesus said, "Follow me." John left the nets, the boat, and his father. John followed Jesus. Instead of finding fish for people to eat, John would be finding people for Jesus to rescue.

Before John could do his new job, he had to learn more about God's good plan. John became one of twelve men called disciples. A disciple is a student of someone who teaches. John was the student. Jesus was the teacher. John learned. Jesus taught.

Every day John would listen to the words Jesus said. Every day John would watch to see what Jesus did. Every day John would learn something new.

John was there when Jesus healed. He watched as Jesus fed thousands of people with a few fish and loaves of bread. John even saw Jesus bring a young girl back to life.

Jesus was more than a teacher. Jesus was a friend. Jesus was unlike anyone John had ever known. Life with Jesus was much better than fishing.

This disciple was a hero of sincerity. To be sincere means John believed what Jesus said. He didn't say one thing to please Jesus and then do something else when Jesus wasn't looking. John meant what he said. He didn't change the way he acted when someone new came into the room. He was truthful and honest. That made him sincere. That's also what made him such a good disciple of Jesus.

Did you know Jesus is still looking for sincere disciples? He's looking for boys and girls just about your size to learn from Him who will take what they learn and use it to help others. He wants someone who looks just like you to be sincere by taking what you learn and letting it change the way you live.

A sincere disciple isn't ashamed of Jesus, no matter who comes into the room. A sincere disciple means what they say and follows what God said. You might just be a sincere hero like John.

Dear God, I want to be sincere when it comes to Jesus. I don't want to act like He doesn't matter around some people and then act as if He's amazing around others. If I love Jesus, I should love Him every moment of every day. Help me learn more about Your Son so I can have my own great adventure by following Him with every part of me. Show me what it means to be sincere. Help me love others the way He loves me. Amen.

• •

BECOMING A HERO

O **What made John a sincere hero?**

O **What did John leave behind so he could follow Jesus?**

O **Do you think you could leave everything to follow Jesus like John did? Why?**

O **What does being sincere mean to you?**

O **What is the opposite of sincerity?**

Loyal and Forgiven

James' Heroic Story

Matthew 4; Mark 14; Acts 12

40

Don't just do the minimum that will get you by. Do your best. Work from the heart for your real Master, for God.

Colossians 3:22 MSG

J ames heard the same two words his brother John had heard. "Follow Me." That's what Jesus had said. That's what James did.

Following Jesus was not usually a burden for James. Following Jesus was God's gift. No human had ever had such close friendship with God's Son before. For so many months there were twelve men listening to God's truth through every word spoken by His Son.

When Jesus asked James and John to follow Him, they didn't know who He was. They had never met Him before. But they followed. They learned. They grew to love Jesus.

When Jesus was looking for disciples, He was looking for those who would be loyal to Him. To be loyal to Jesus was to faithfully support Him. James was a loyal hero. Where Jesus went, James followed. When Jesus spoke, James listened. What Jesus taught, James learned.

During the last supper Jesus would eat before dying on the cross, He asked James, John, and Peter to keep Him company while He prayed. The three disciples didn't ask questions. They followed Jesus. James had no idea this would be the last time he would see Jesus before He died.

While the three waited for Jesus, they grew sleepy. They were confused when another disciple named Judas brought soldiers who arrested Jesus. For a moment James forgot to be loyal. For a moment he thought he would also be hurt. For a moment James ran away with his brother John and his friend Peter.

Jesus was left alone with men who thought what He taught was foolish. He was left alone with no one to teach, so He remained quiet. He was left alone to remember that what was about to happen was why He had come. Jesus would die. James would be sad. The greatest teacher the world had ever known would go away. Or would He?

The disciples met together after Jesus died. They remembered what Jesus had taught them. James rediscovered his loyalty when Jesus arrived. He was no longer dead. His sacrifice paid the price for the bad choice James had made to run away. Sadness was replaced with joy.

Forgiveness changes things. Forgiveness offers freedom from guilt. Forgiveness inspires friendship. Forgiveness was what Jesus offered, and James became loyal once more.

Being a hero of loyalty is important for anyone who wants to learn from Jesus. His lessons are perfect. His plans are better than yours. His love always brings freedom.

Dear God, You have always been loyal to me, even when I don't follow Your plan. Your loyalty is why You paid for my sin choices by dying on a cross. You came to show what being loyal looks like. James learned a lot about being loyal. Help me learn that being loyal to You is a perfect choice. Amen.

* *

BECOMING A HERO

O   **Why was it easy for James to be loyal to Jesus?**

O   **Why might it have been hard for James to be loyal to Jesus?**

O   **How loyal to Jesus do you think you are?**

O   **Why do you think it is important to know that Jesus can forgive you when you aren't loyal?**

O   **What is the opposite of being loyal?**

41

An Unexpected Friendship

Luke's Heroic Story

THE BOOKS OF LUKE & ACTS

A friend is always loyal.

PROVERBS 17:17 NLT

Some people thought Luke didn't belong. He seemed like a stranger at a family reunion. Luke hadn't always followed God, but God had invited Luke to be part of His family. People were surprised.

Luke was asked to do something that had never been done before. God asked Luke to write two books of the Bible. Every other book was written by someone who was part of the family of Israel. This meant something important. God had always invested in the lives of His family, but because God loved everyone, He invited every man, woman, boy, and girl to become part of His family.

Luke was a doctor. He used medicines from the things God created to help people get well. Luke wanted his patients to be healthy, but he also wanted them to be forgiven. He wanted them to follow God.

God sent Luke to talk to people who had seen the miracles of Jesus. He listened to grand stories that amazed him. There were so many stories, memories, and miracles. The book of Luke became a collection of eyewitness accounts of people who had met Jesus face-to-face.

Luke shared the story of the shepherds who went to see Jesus in a manger, the story of those who watched Him die on the cross, and the story of those who spoke to Jesus after He rose from the dead.

This stranger to the family of Israel learned about Jesus from people who had actually spent time with Him. Luke became a trusted new family member, and he wrote about the very earliest days of the Christian faith after Jesus returned to God. This history book is called Acts.

It's not often that an outcast physician can become a trusted keeper of the greatest story ever, but that's what happened when God showed Luke where to go next and what to do that would honor Him. Luke accepted God's friendship and became a hero.

Maybe God brought an outsider into His family so people could see that God came for all people in all places for all time. God showed regular people that friendship with Him was possible and was something He wanted.

God doesn't just love *some* people. God doesn't leave people out. He loved Luke. He loves you.

Take His gift of friendship and share it with someone who needs a friend.

Dear God, thanks for making it possible for me to be part of Your family. I didn't do anything to deserve Your love. I have broken Your rules, but You love me enough to make an impossible friendship possible. Thanks for showing me that a doctor who had never been a part of Your family became a friend and You gave him a job. I can't wait to see what You want me to do. Thanks. Amen.

• •

BECOMING A HERO

○ Why do you think people might have been surprised that God chose Luke as a hero of friendship?

○ How many books of the Bible did Luke write?

○ Why do you think God wants to be friends with you?

○ What did you learn from Luke that will help you be a friend to others?

○ What is the opposite of friendship?

42

True Worship

Mary and Martha's Heroic Story
Luke 10:38–42

*Let us be thankful and please
God by worshiping him.*

Hebrews 12:28 NLT

Jesus was going to stay in the home of two sisters. One sister was named Mary, and she loved to spend time learning from Jesus. The other sister was named Martha, and she wanted to make sure her home was clean and the food was excellent.

Mary didn't understand why Martha was so worried about how the house looked. Martha didn't understand why Mary couldn't see that a clean house was her way of honoring Jesus.

When Jesus arrived, Mary sat down to listen to His words. She honored Him by paying attention. She cared enough to learn what was important to Him.

When Jesus arrived, Martha was in the kitchen making good food. She honored Jesus by caring for His needs. She cared enough to make sure Jesus was comfortable in her home.

Who honored Jesus the most? Who was a hero of worship?

Jesus was thankful for Martha for the way she cared for His needs. Jesus was thankful for Mary for wanting to spend time learning from Him. He accepted both as gifts of worship. He wanted the sisters to understand they had both been a blessing to Him. He also wanted Martha to understand that her way of worship wasn't the only way to worship. Jesus complimented Mary because she understood the time with Him was more important than a tasty meal and clean house.

Martha wanted Jesus to tell Mary to help. She must have felt badly when Jesus told her He just wanted to spend time with them. Martha was looking at what she could do to make Jesus happy. Mary wanted to spend time with the One who offered joy.

Both sisters worshipped Jesus, but He made sure we would know which type of worship is more honoring to Him.

Both sisters are heroes of worship, but even the best of heroes keep learning—and so can you.

Worship pays attention to Jesus, not what others are doing. Worship helps you learn about Jesus without trying to get Him to notice how helpful you can be. Worship honors Jesus without asking to be honored by Jesus.

You can be a hero of worship. Just remember that Jesus has already done everything needed to be your friend. You can't impress Him or make Him love you more than He already does. Take the time to get to know Him, learn from Him, and honor Him with all you are, all He made you to be, in every thought you think, and in everything you do.

Dear God, sometimes I want to impress You. You're so amazing, and I want You to notice me. Help me remember that You have always loved me more than anyone ever could. I want to honor You by learning everything I can about You. I want to serve You but not because I'm trying to get Your attention—I already have that. Thank You. Amen.

. . . .

BECOMING A HERO

○ **Why do you think Martha was so upset with Mary?**

○ **What did Jesus say was more important when people worship Him?**

○ **Why do you think it's easy to believe that you need to impress God to make Him happy with you?**

○ **Why do you think Jesus said it was better to spend time with Him?**

○ **What is the opposite of worship?**

43

A Story of Acceptance
The Good Samaritan's Heroic Story
Luke 10:30–37

In Christ's family there can be no division into Jew and non-Jew, slave and free, male and female. Among us you are all equal. That is, we are all in a common relationship with Jesus Christ.

GALATIANS 3:28 MSG

Luke didn't come from the family of Israel, but God welcomed him into His family. Luke wrote down the history of Jesus by talking to people who met Jesus. Luke learned that Jesus loved to tell stories.

The good Samaritan story caught Luke's attention. This was the story of a man who helped when no one else would. He cared when others were too busy. He accepted when others walked by.

The story Jesus told was from His imagination. It was memorable. The story had a surprise ending.

There once was a man who left Jerusalem on his way to Jericho. He hadn't gotten far when outlaws took his money, knocked him to the ground, and left him hurt, alone, and needing help.

Two men walked by who could have helped, should have helped, but did not help. A priest and a man who worked in the temple saw the hurting man, knew he needed help, but were too busy to stop.

The man lay on the side of the road wondering if help would ever come. Then he heard the sound of a horse and then footsteps, and then he saw something that made him wonder if things could get any worse. The footsteps belonged to a Samaritan. No one seemed to like people from Samaria. No one from Samaria seemed to like people from Israel. The man on the side of the road did not believe the Samaritan would help.

Imagine his surprise when the man stopped and looked over his wounds, wrapped them in cloth, and took him to get help. The Samaritan paid for everything the hurt man needed to get well.

Luke heard that Jesus told those who followed Him to treat all people the same way the Samaritan treated the stranger.

The Samaritan was a hero of acceptance. He didn't ask about what family the man came from. He didn't ask if the man could pay him back. He didn't say kind words and walk away. He saw a man in need—and he helped.

Christianity isn't a club you can join if other people in the club like you. Christianity is a gift from God. He's always wanted to bring people together and teach them to really care about each other.

Dear God, You used Luke, an outsider, to talk about a Samaritan, another outsider. You must have wanted people to know that You came to do something special for anyone. You could have used kings and wise men to share Your message, but You must have known I would accept Your message better from regular people. Thanks for making sure I got the message. Help me help others. Amen.

• •

BECOMING A HERO

○ **Why do you think it was important that it was the Samaritan who helped the man who was hurt?**

○ **How did the Samaritan show he cared?**

○ **Have you ever been around someone who needed help, but you decided not to help? Why?**

○ **Jesus called the Samaritan a good neighbor. How can you be a good neighbor to someone today?**

○ **What is the opposite of acceptance?**

44

Late-Night Learning

Nicodemus' Heroic Story

JOHN 3; 7:50–51

Intelligent people are always
ready to learn. Their ears are
open for knowledge.

PROVERBS 18:15 NLT

Jesus is never pleased with people who show off. Pharisees were known for showing off. If you went to church, Pharisees made sure you knew they went to church more. If you prayed, they made sure you knew they prayed more important prayers. If you followed God, they made sure you were aware they were better followers. Pharisees believed they were God's favorite people.

Pharisees believed God loved them more and accepted them above others. They thought they had the right to look down on everyone else. Jesus told them this attitude kept them from God. The Pharisees hated Jesus because He did not honor them as heroes.

There was one Pharisee who became a hero. Nicodemus was a hero of learning. While other Pharisees wanted to make Jesus look foolish, Nicodemus wanted to know more about what Jesus was teaching. If the other Pharisees knew what Nicodemus was thinking, they might have told him he couldn't be a Pharisee anymore.

One night Nicodemus came to see Jesus. He honored Jesus by calling Him a rabbi, which means teacher. Most Pharisees wanted to teach Jesus. Nicodemus believed Jesus could teach him.

Jesus told Nicodemus that he had been born once and he had used his life to try to be as good as possible, but he still sinned. The Pharisees had self-discipline. They did good things. They obeyed many of God's rules. Jesus said it would never be enough. Jesus told Nicodemus he would need to be born again.

This was a new idea for Nicodemus. He had never heard of anyone being born twice. To be born again was the symbol of becoming a brand-new member of God's family.

Jesus would become the sacrifice that made this possible. Nicodemus would have a lot to think about in the days after his visit with Jesus. Nicodemus understood that Jesus was a teacher worth listening to.

You might think you can make God like you more, but you can't. You can obey more of God's rules than anyone you know, but when you break even one rule, you have sinned. You can't repay God for your bad choices by making good choices. You need to be forgiven. You need God to rescue you. You need Jesus to take your sin and get rid of it.

God doesn't compare you to other people; He compares you to

Jesus. He was perfect, and God accepts His perfection as full payment for your sin. You win. God sees you as forgiven and clean.

Dear God, You want me to love my Christian family. That's hard to do when I keep comparing myself to them. Sometimes I think I'm doing pretty well. Sometimes I feel like everyone is doing better than I am. Help me to learn that I can love others better when I accept Your forgiveness and love. Amen.

- -

BECOMING A HERO

O **Why do you think Nicodemus makes a good hero of learning?**

O **Why was it important that Nicodemus called Jesus "Teacher"?**

O **Why is learning more about Jesus important?**

O **Why does accepting Jesus' forgiveness help you accept others?**

O **What is the opposite of learning?**

45

Called to Serve
Simon of Cyrene's Heroic Story
MARK 15

Never be lazy, but work hard and serve the Lord enthusiastically.
ROMANS 12:11 NLT

Simon didn't live in Jerusalem. He lived in Africa. His home was in Cyrene. He was a guest visiting Jerusalem with his sons.

Maybe Simon was in Jerusalem on business. Maybe he was there to stay with family or friends. Simon was about to meet Jesus.

Simon had been out in the countryside with his sons when Jesus was condemned to die. He was walking into town when Jesus was carrying his cross down the city streets. Simon was just one more person wondering what this wounded man had done. Then a soldier called Simon forward.

Jesus was struggling to carry the cross, but the soldier was impatient and didn't want to carry the cross for Jesus. He commanded Simon to carry it.

Simon's sons stayed together as their father lifted the cross and walked beside Jesus. Simon knew this man was going to die on the same cross he was asked to carry. The two walked quietly as people laughed and called Jesus horrible names.

This was not what Simon expected. He didn't come to Jerusalem to carry a cross. He didn't see this visit as an opportunity to walk with a condemned man. Hadn't he spent the morning with his sons? Hadn't he been a good father? Hadn't he obeyed the law?

Simon may have been angry that he was asked to carry the cross, but Simon was a servant hero before he really understood who he was serving. Simon didn't understand why serving Jesus was so important. Perhaps God had led Simon from Cyrene to Jerusalem because He knew Simon would help.

You know more about Jesus today than Simon did. You have more reason to serve than Simon did. You know whom you serve—Jesus. You know why you serve Him—He's given you a job to do. He knows you can help.

You can serve Jesus because you love Him. You can love Him because He loved you first. He loved you first because you needed to know what love looked like. When you know what love looks like, you can serve Jesus well.

When you serve God, you will be asked to serve others. Helping people is a way to show that God's love is changing you. You stop thinking about all the things you can get and you start living for ways to help God change the world one person at a time. Serving is a kindness, and kindness is like the gift of water on a hot day—refreshing and just what you need.

Dear God, You made everything—and it is perfect.
You gave me the chance to choose. I don't always obey
Your rules. I have not always been a servant hero, but I
would like to be useful to You. You can do anything.
You don't even need my help. I am thankful You want
my help. Help me serve You because I love You. Amen.

• •

BECOMING A HERO

O **Why do you think Simon would have been surprised to be asked to carry Jesus' cross?**

O **Why would it be hard not to know why you were being asked to serve?**

O **How do you feel when you are asked to serve others?**

O **What makes it easier to think you should be served?**

O **What is the opposite of serving?**

Generous Gifts

Joseph of Arimathea's Heroic Story

JOHN 19

46

God loves it when the giver delights in the giving.

2 CORINTHIANS 9:7 MSG

You've learned about Joseph who was the son of Jacob. He was sold as a slave in Egypt. God used him to save his family during a time when there was very little food. You've learned about Joseph, the husband of Mary. He was responsible and took care of Jesus. There was another Joseph, and he was a hero of generosity. We know him as Joseph of Arimathea.

This Joseph was a member of the high council. People respected Joseph. Some religious leaders didn't seem to really follow God. Joseph wanted to see the Savior God had promised. He wanted to honor the one called Messiah.

Joseph had seen what it was like when leaders who were supposed to love God made all kinds of plans to hurt Jesus. He was betrayed. He was arrested. He was listening when the people yelled, "Crucify him."

Joseph knew Jesus was punished and would soon die on a cross. Joseph knew Jesus was innocent and what was being done to Him was very wrong.

Joseph felt awe when the skies grew dark. *Jesus just died.*

Rain fell. *Jesus hung silently.*

The earth shook. *It was over.*

Joseph knew what he needed to do. He went to see Governor Pilate. He asked if he could have the body of Jesus so He could be buried. In that moment, Joseph of Arimathea became a hero of generosity. A large round stone was rolled away from the opening of a tomb owned by Joseph. This would be where God's Son would be buried. This would be the place where soldiers would stay in order to stop anyone from taking the body of Jesus away.

Three days later Jesus no longer needed the tomb. Jesus fought death and won. He was alive again! He said that would happen. Jesus paid the price for the sin choices of Joseph of Arimathea. Jesus paid the price for your sin choices. That part of Jesus that was just like God could not die. The stone over the entrance to the tomb was rolled away, and Jesus left death behind.

A hero of generosity is someone who gives without thinking they will get something in return. They share without seeing the gift as paying someone back for being kind. They help because someone needs help.

Joseph gave Jesus what he had. Jesus gave everything so Joseph could be close to God. This is the best story of generosity in the Bible.

Dear God, thank You for helping me see what it looks like to be generous. Joseph cared about Jesus and helped in a way no one else thought of. He was available when Jesus had a need. Jesus is available whenever I have a need. You have always been generous. Help me to be more like You. Amen.

• •

BECOMING A HERO

O **Why is it right to think of Joseph of Arimathea as a hero of generosity?**

O **Who has always been the perfect example of generosity?**

O **Can you remember a time when you were generous? What happened?**

O **How can being generous change the way you think?**

O **What is the opposite of generosity?**

47

Gratitude after Attitude

Peter's Heroic Story

Matthew 14, 16, 18, 26; John 21

> Be thankful in all circumstances, for this is God's will for you who belong to Christ Jesus.
>
> 1 Thessalonians 5:18 nlt

Peter was a disciple. He liked to make promises. He wanted to be Jesus' favorite.

The possibility of adventure was something Peter liked. One night when Jesus prayed, Peter and the other disciples got into a boat and headed to the opposite shore. It wasn't long before a storm made it feel like the boat was going to tip over. That's when the disciples noticed Jesus was walking on the water. He wasn't swimming. He wasn't rowing a different boat. Jesus was actually walking on top of the water.

Peter thought that was amazing. He asked Jesus if he could walk on the water, too. Peter had never walked on water. He didn't know anyone but Jesus who had ever done that. Usually people who tried to walk on water sank. Jesus told Peter to get out of the boat and walk to him. Peter took a few steps and stopped. He suddenly felt afraid. He stopped walking and started sinking. Jesus had to rescue Peter. It wouldn't be the last time.

Peter tried to make himself appear better than the other disciples. Most people found it hard to forgive someone even once. Peter thought that seven times would be pretty good. Instead of Jesus telling the other disciples they should be more like Peter, Jesus told them they should forgive and stop counting. Peter would learn he would need to be forgiven by Jesus many times.

When Jesus was betrayed and taken away to be killed, Peter ran away. When people said they had seen Peter with Jesus, he lied and said he had no idea who Jesus was. Peter seemed to make a mess of so many things.

But when Jesus rose from the dead and wanted the disciples to understand His plan for their future, Jesus wanted to speak to Peter. Maybe Peter thought he was in trouble. He couldn't blame Jesus for being ashamed of him. He deserved whatever he got. Jesus surprised Peter. He told him that he would build the Church using Peter. He wanted Peter to be a leader. He wanted Peter to follow Him once more.

Jesus had forgiven Peter for things that usually end friendship. Jesus told Peter that His future plans included him. Peter learned that when he was forgiven he was grateful. He became a hero of gratitude.

When you make the choice to follow Jesus, you will not get it 100 percent right the first time. Making good choices can take time. It will always take God's help—and He will help. Being grateful is heroic.

Dear Jesus, You must be very patient. Every time I make the wrong choice, You offer to forgive me. Every time I make promises and break them, You remind me that I need to follow Your plan. Every time I am impatient and want something now, You are patient with me. Even when I don't always cooperate, thank You for never giving up on me. Amen.

· ·

BECOMING A HERO

O **Do you think Peter liked to show off? Why?**

O **Why did Peter need to be forgiven?**

O **How have you ever acted like Peter?**

O **What is your response when someone breaks a promise?**

O **What is the opposite of gratitude?**

Becoming Teachable
Paul's Heroic Story
ACTS 9–12

48

Instruct the wise and they will be wiser still; teach the righteous and they will add to their learning.

PROVERBS 9:9 NIV

Pharisees were very proud of how well they followed God. They tried to make other people appear less important. They stayed away from anyone who wasn't like them. Paul the apostle was a Pharisee. He'd even gone to school to become the best Pharisee possible.

Paul had heard about Jesus. Everything he'd heard about him was bad. He had never met Jesus before He died on the cross, but the Pharisees were upset because people were still following Jesus' teachings. They thought people would stop following Jesus after He was gone. Paul was willing to hurt people if that meant they would stop following Jesus.

One day something impossible happened. Paul was surprised. He had a visit from Jesus as he walked along the Damascus road. Paul was blinded by a bright light. He fell to the ground, and Jesus asked Paul why he was trying to hurt Him.

Paul thought Jesus had died. Paul never believed Jesus rose from the dead. Now Jesus was talking to him. Had Paul been wrong about Jesus? How could someone who had died speak again? Had Paul been making a mistake in trying to stop people from believing in Jesus?

Paul followed the directions Jesus had given him. He went to meet a man named Ananias who would pray for him. Jesus had Paul's attention. For the first time in Paul's life, he was praying to Jesus—not trying to hurt His family.

Jesus used Ananias to help Paul see again. Most people were afraid of Paul. Jesus saw what Paul could become and helped point him in the right direction.

Paul was a Pharisee. He was an expert in Jewish law. But Jesus asked him to take God's plan of forgiveness and rescue to people who were not Jewish. It didn't seem like this was a good job for Paul, but God can use unlikely people to help with His wonderful plans.

Paul liked to learn, but there was a lot to know about Jesus, the Rescuer. Paul shared what he learned and kept learning. Paul followed Jesus and kept following. Paul wrote what he was taught and kept writing. Paul had been an enemy of God's greatest plan but became someone God could use to share His love.

Paul was a teachable hero. He had to learn the truth about God's plan, share God's good news, and help train others to share His wonderful story.

God can teach you. He can help you understand what is true. You can love others by telling them His truth.

Dear God, You want people who can learn it all—not people who think they know it all. Help me be a learn-it-all follower. I want to be teachable. I want the things I learn to help me understand You better and help me make better choices. Thank You for being willing to teach. I want to be a good student. Amen.

• •

BECOMING A HERO

O **Why would it have been hard for people to believe Paul was really following Jesus?**

O **How did Paul show he was teachable?**

O **Why do you think it is hard to spend time with people who are filled with pride?**

O **What can you do today to show God you're willing to learn more from Him?**

O **What is the opposite of teachable?**

49

A Friend to Encourage

Barnabas' Heroic Story

ACTS 13–14

I pray that God, the source of hope, will fill you completely with joy and peace because you trust in him. Then you will overflow with confident hope through the power of the Holy Spirit.

ROMANS 15:13 NLT

God used the apostle Paul to write the words you just read. This verse is one example of how Paul encouraged others. God did a wonderful thing in Paul's life, but Paul also had a friend who helped show him how encouragement can change the way he looked at life.

Barnabas was a man known as the Son of Encouragement. It sounds like he would have been a great friend. It sounds like it would be nice to spend time with Barnabas. It sounds like he was just the right man to help Paul move from being someone who hurt Christians to someone who could teach them.

Sometimes when a person makes wrong choices for a long time, it can be hard for people to think that they've really changed when they start making good choices. Barnabas knew this, so he took Paul away from the people who couldn't believe he had really changed. The two went on missionary trips far away from the people who could only remember Paul as someone who hated Christians.

While Paul traveled for a few years, he learned more about Jesus. He became more interested in sharing God's message with those who needed to hear it. He helped start new churches. Barnabas stayed with him and encouraged him. Paul needed a good friend who believed that God was making him into something much better than most people remembered. Barnabas was the friend Paul needed.

For many years Paul and Barnabas were the best of friends. Barnabas taught Paul what he knew about Jesus. Barnabas encouraged Paul to keep walking toward the finish line of faith. Barnabas helped Paul show others the difference God can make in a person who is willing to learn why the change God can make is so important.

Spend time with someone who will encourage you to become more like Jesus. You will gain a friend, improve your friendship with Jesus, and become a better friend for others.

God created encouragement so you wouldn't have to be alone. God knew you would have bad days and would need someone to help you. God sends people to help so you can remember He wants you to be encouraged.

Barnabas followed Jesus before he met Paul. He could have stayed away from Paul because people didn't trust him. God chose Barnabas to help Paul. Today you get to see what a hero of encouragement does to help others.

Dear God, help me use the encouragement of others to become closer to You. Help me learn to encourage others so they can become close to You. Help me remember that to be encouraged I need to be around people who encourage me. You say that friends are important. Encouraging friends are the best kinds of friends. Amen.

• •

BECOMING A HERO

○ **Why do you think Paul needed an encouraging friend?**

○ **How did Barnabas help Paul?**

○ **Name a friend who encourages you. What do they do that encourages you?**

○ **Why do you think encouragement is so important to God?**

○ **What is the opposite of encouragement?**

About the Author

Glenn A. Hascall is an accomplished writer with credits in more than one hundred books, including titles from Thomas Nelson, Bethany House, and Regal. His writing has appeared in numerous publications around the globe. He's also an award-winning broadcaster, lending his voice to animation and audio drama projects.

Continue the Fun with...

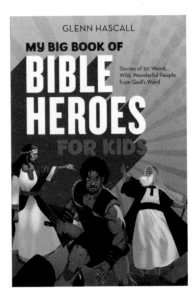

My Big Book of Bible Heroes for Kids

This fully-illustrated book highlights the stories of 50 weird, wild, and wonderful Bible heroes from God's Word. Readers of all ages will be captivated by the action-packed art that pops off the page while they learn about how God has used ordinary people to accomplish great things.

Paperback / 978-1-63409-315-6 / $14.99